HOW I BECAME A SPIRITUALIST

By

Paul Shave

CON-PSY PUBLICATIONS

First Edition

© Paul Shave
2014

This book is copyrighted under the Berne Convention.
All rights reserved.
No part of this book may be reproduced or utilised in any form or by any means, electronic or mechanical, including photocopying, recording, or by any information storage and retrieval system, without permission in writing from the publisher. Except for the purpose of reviewing or criticism, as permitted under the Copyright Act of 1956.

Published by
CON-PSY PUBLICATIONS

P.O. BOX 14,
GREENFORD,
MIDDLESEX, UB6 0UF.

ISBN 978 1 898680 71 0

CONTENTS

PREFACE	7
CHAPTER ONE	9
CHAPTER TWO	19
CHAPTER THREE	23
CHAPTER FOUR	31
CHAPTER FIVE	38
CHAPTER SIX	49
CHAPTER SEVEN	54
CHAPTER EIGHT	58
CHAPTER NINE	66
CHAPTER TEN	76
CHAPTER ELEVEN	89
APPENDIX	99
ARTICLE 1: RECEIVING A MESSAGE FROM A MEDIUM	99
ARTICLE 2: FURTHER THOUGHTS ON RECEIVING A MESSAGE FROM A MEDIUM	101

PREFACE

This is a book about the events in my life that have influenced me, not just in becoming a Spiritualist, but also how my views on life and religion have changed over the years.

It is not meant to be a biography, because I confess that I have been a person who has not recorded events and happenings that have taken place throughout my life, either on paper or photographically. I have lived life very much from day-to-day and have never, for instance, kept a diary recording daily events. I am, therefore, writing this book relying mostly on my memory to recall the things that have been of importance to me.

Although, as stated above, I am not writing biographically, I will endeavour to include as much as I can remember concerning such things as my family/friends and my place and date of birth, plus any other relevant facts that I consider to be of help in understanding the events that have happened to me and my family throughout our lives.

The reason I am writing this book is partly in response to a number of friends and family members who, on hearing the things and situations that I have experienced through out my life, have responded by saying: "You should write a book".

In considering their suggestion, I decided that not only is it a good idea for me to do as they suggested, but that in doing so I may also be of help to people who are searching for the answers, to questions such as who are we and what is the purpose of our lives hear on Earth etc?

We all learn many things as we progress through our lives and much of what we learn is by hearing of what other people have experienced, as well as the things that happen to each of us personally. It is, therefore, obvious to me that whatever I can do to help other people to have a more enlightened understanding as to what life is all about by writing this book, is not only desirable but is a duty that I should carry out to the best of my ability.

If as a result of writing this book I am able to help even just one person to navigate their way through the many challenges of their life that they will inevitably face then I shall feel more than satisfied.

The views which I express in this book are my own personal beliefs and are not meant to represent any of the Spiritualist organisations.

CHAPTER ONE

I was born on the 1st of July 1936 in Morden, Surrey at 17 Easby Crescent on the St Helier council estate. I was named Paul by my mother and Edward (my second name), which was suggested by my father. He said it came to him because in that same year Edward The Eighth was due to be the next king, but more appropriately I was the eighth child to be born as a result of his marriage to my mother. At the time of my birth the family consisted of my father and mother plus three brothers and three sisters. There was a fourth brother who had died many years earlier, thus I am the eighth child of their marriage.

I am the only one of their children born in Surrey. All of my brothers and sisters were born in London, as was my father. My mother was born in Kent.

The nearest brother to me age wise was John. He was eight years my senior. He and all my other brothers and sisters have joined our mum and dad in the world of Spirit.

My mum and dad were blessed with having their first child on the 2nd of July 1916 and their last child, which, of course, was me, on the 1st of July 1936. This is remarkable in that it was only one day short of being exactly twenty years to the day between their first born and myself.

I think my parents can be justly proud to have brought up a caring, sharing family that was reasonably close knit, with a good attitude not only to one another but also towards the community around them and to Mankind in general. My parents were so grateful that the whole family came through the Second World War without loss.

My parents both came through their childhood years in the latter part of the Victorian era in comparative poverty and were also both children of broken marriages.

It would have been easy for them, considering the conditions they found themselves in, to have lost their way on the treadmill of daily life.

There is not a lot more that I wish to write about my family's early history, including my early years as a child etc. because, as I said in my preface to this book, I have not written it as a biography of my life or as a family history but rather as an account of events that led me towards becoming a Spiritualist.

I am, therefore, going to advance forward in time to the year 1956, which was when I met the young woman who was later to become my wife. Her name was Dorothy, but she much preferred to be called Dee.

Our first meeting was at Harrods, the well known London department store. She was working in the engineering office and she was the first person I saw when I walked into the office to arrange to resume my duties as a trainee engineer after a two year absence in the Royal Air Force. For me, it was a case of love at first sight and very soon I was able to arrange our first date.

After courting for just over two years, we got married on the 1st of March 1958 and for the first two-and-a-half years we lived in the top half of my mother and father's council house in Morden, Surrey.

It was quite a common thing at that time for newlyweds to live in part of their parents' houses if they were unable to afford or find a place of their own in which to start their married life.

Whilst living there, we had our first child, who was born in St Helier Hospital, Carshalton, Surrey. Our first baby was a girl and we named her Deena Lesley.

Both my parents and Dee's parents were thrilled, of course and so were we. However, it soon became obvious to all concerned that it would be better for us all if Dee and I could find a place of our own in which to live and bring up our daughter.

We were able to find a two bedroomed ground floor flat in Tooting and although there was no bathroom and the toilet was outside, we were happy to be able to find a place that included a garden at the rear that was offered at a rent that was affordable to us.

We lived there several years during which time we were blessed with two more children. The children now consisted of Deena and her two brothers, Glen and Michael.

It was also whilst living at that address that both Dee and I were influenced in different ways to change our views regarding how we thought about religion.

I considered myself at that time to be an agnostic because I was not convinced of the teachings of Christianity which I had received at school, but at the same time I was not happy to accept the view held by atheists that there is no God.

Dee, for her part, was happy to be considered as a Christian, although she did not attend any church.

I think it was in about the year 1960 that we both started to think differently regarding our beliefs. In my case it was as a result of having been given two books to read whilst in Dee's case it was as a result of becoming influenced by an acquaintance who, in being a committed, Jehovah's Witness, considered it her duty to try, over the next two years, to get her to join her religion.

Dee told me that although she was impressed with the beliefs of the Witnesses, she felt that their teaching regarding their rule of not accepting blood transfusions, because of what is written in the Bible, could not be justified to her satisfaction. And it was mainly for that reason that she felt unable to join her friend in her religion. At the same time as she was studying with the Witnesses, Dee became pregnant for the third time. This made her even more uncertain with regards to becoming a member of the J.W. organisation because expecting a third child only added to her doubts regarding their ruling concerning blood transfusions. This had bothered her for some time and now, with the expected increase in her responsibilities, she felt even more strongly that her duty towards her children to ensure that their welfare was safe in her hands was now even more important to her.

When she expressed her feelings on the matter to her friend, she answered with great conviction that she must accept the teaching because it is recorded in the Bible and it was, therefore, a direct command from God that we must not accept blood. It was also suggested to her by her friend that it is highly unlikely for her ever to have to face the decision concerning blood transfusion because God only presents us with challenges that we are able to cope with.

Dee had heard all this before from her friend and was no more convinced on hearing it yet again than she than had been on the several previous occasions. Neither was she prepared to accept that every word written in the Bible is the word of God and must be accepted without exception as the truth, as is believed by Jehovah's Witnesses.

Dee respected her friend and to some extent admired her dedication to her chosen religion but she still felt unable to join her in her beliefs.

Some months later our second son was born in The Wier Hospital in Balham. His body was found to be totally jaundiced, which made his little body yellow from head to toe. We were advised that the condition was life-threatening and was strongly advised by the surgical team that if we would consent to a blood transfusion, which would entail *exchanging all of his own blood for fresh donated blood*, there was a good chance he would survive the operation and make a full recovery.

Of course, Dee and I both consented to the transfusion and Michael, as we had by now named him, had the procedure that had been advised and went on to make a full recovery.

Needless to say, from that moment on Dee's decision as to whether or not to become a Jehovah's Witness was put on indefinite hold.

As mentioned earlier, I had also changed my religious beliefs after having been given two books on two separate occasions by two different members of my family.

The first book was given to me by my oldest brother Geoff. It was entitled 'Life and Teachings of the Masters of the Far East', written by Baird T. Spalding. (Volume 1).

I found out some time later that there were another five volumes, making six in all and some years later I obtained them all.

Baird T.Spalding wrote the book to record his experiences, which he shared with ten other people over a period of some three-and-a-half years as a member of a research party to the Far East in 1894.

During their time there they came into contact with the Great Masters of the Himalayas, who helped them by not only helping them with the translation of their records but, more importantly, they also allowed the party to share their lives and customs. This meant that they were able, on each and every day that they shared with them, to personally observe how these people applied themselves to the task of understanding the great Law of Life and how it affected what they were able to achieve.

I found the book to be very interesting from several aspects and very enlightening in so many ways and on the completion of my reading of the book, I also realised that the main thing that I had learnt from the experience was that I now realised that there is much more to the human race than the physical aspect. Most importantly, I by now (having read some of the experiences related by the author) was beginning to realise that all men and women are spiritual individuals first but, in addition to that fact, that everyone also has a physical body. This is different to how most people think because they tend to think of the spiritual and the physical the other way round, i.e. that each individual has a physical body that also has a spirit within.

A few years later, as a result of investigating Spiritualist philosophy, I would learn of how it is only the physical body that ceases to exist at the time of death and that the spirit of each person continues to live on.

Looking back to that moment in time, I was beginning to leave my agnostic view of life behind me, although I was not yet aware of it.

A few months after being given the afore-mentioned book by my brother, I was given the second book, which came to me as a gift from my brother-in-law, Jack and it was this book that would prove to be the turning point for me on my religious journey. It is one of the last books by the famous historical figure Thomas Paine. The title of the book is 'THE AGE OF REASON', which he wrote in spite of his being at the time in prison in France during the French revolution.

He had intended to publish his thoughts on religion for some years and was already well known for his political pamphlets and books and also for his activities in politics in England, America and France. He was also involved with the revolutions that took place in both of the latter two nations mentioned above.

In France, the political group known as the Girondin (of which Paine was a member) fell out of favour with the authorities. Paine was imprisoned and was in constant danger of execution. This motivated him to write 'THE AGE OF REASON' and so without further delay and in spite of being in prison and in fear for his life, he wrote part one of the book. On his release in the year 1794, he was able to write part two.

The writing of part one was a greater achievement than the writing of part two because he was not allowed the benefit of having a Bible with him in his prison cell to refer to and as a result he had to rely solely on his memory, which proved to be outstanding. You see, he was brought up as a Quaker in his childhood and therefore had a very considerable knowledge of the Bible.

In his book, he made the case for Deism, which is the belief in God, but not in revelation. He declared that the evidence for the existence of God is far more powerful and reasonable through the *evidence and the wonders of the universe and creation and its unchanging natural laws* than the evidence found in any book on the subject of religion could ever be, not least because any book that is said to be evidential and factual must of necessity be able to be verified as being so.

This is particularly important in the case of religious books, including the Bible, because of the importance of the subject matter they contain. These books are faced even more with the need to satisfy the question of proof of their authenticity that any books that are being presented as factual are faced with. In addition to this, on its completion, any written work, whether it is fact or fiction, faces the same challenges, which are as follows: Any book on its completion could be suppressed or destroyed or copied inaccurately (deliberately or otherwise). Further to this, there is the question of misunderstanding its contents, which is in turn linked to interpreting the contents *without prejudice*. In addition, of course, there is the undeniable fact that any written work is totally ineffective if it is never seen by anyone. These requirements are, of course, even more necessary in the case of religious books because they are usually presented to the reader, as THE WORD OF GOD.

Let us now consider whether it is reasonable to be asked to accept The Bible as the word of God, or indeed for that matter any other religious work which claims that same authority for its contents. I say no, it is not reasonable. Not just because of the reasons regarding vulnerability that I have already outlined above, but also because of two further questions that must be able to be answered in the affirmative before the Bible can be said to be the truth.

The first question is this: Could the Bible be of any use in any way to the world's population that was in existence before it was compiled (which incidentally took many years to complete)? The answer is clearly no, because when a book of any kind is completed it needs to be available to be read and understood to be of any value to the reader. It therefore follows that all those people who died before the book was written cannot have received any benefit from it contents whatsoever because the book had yet to be written. The second question to be considered is this: Even allowing for the fact that all religious writings came into being comparatively recently in the long history of man, would its contents be of value to the majority of the population at any given time after its completion? The answer is again, no, because even up to the present time there are millions of people throughout the world who are ignorant of its contents because of it having been denied to them. This lack of knowledge of the Bible could be for many reasons. Here are just a few: Prevention of access to its contents through not being allowed to read it by the actions of opposing self-interested parties. These parties could be political or religious or some other group of people who have their own ulterior motives for not allowing people to have free access to the book and its teachings. As a result of this lack of availability of the book many people would be completely unaware of its contents.

It may be, of course, that they are just geographically unable to have satisfactory contact with their fellow humankind and as a result remain ignorant of the rest of the world's many facets of life, which would, of course, include books. There are many cases of communities and even nations that are, even to the present day, isolated from civilisation in this way.

The last fact that I want to remind the reader of is that even now, with all of the progress that Mankind has achieved right up to this present time, there are still millions of people who are illiterate throughout the world. For these people, books of any description are of no possible use whatsoever. They are, in most cases, people who are too busy trying to scratch a living and trying to survive to be too concerned about increasing their knowledge in any particular way. And it is, of course, too often the case that they don't have the opportunity to do so, even if they want to.

I hope I have given you some very sound reasons as to why I am unable to accept any *written* word as the word of God and why I prefer the unchanging laws of God's creation and the universe to satisfy my thirst for religious knowledge.

I suggest that it is totally illogical and unreasonable that God, whom I consider to be perfection, would use such an inadequate method as the written word for communicating to Mankind the fact of His existence. I believe that the Almighty has equipped every species of His creation with just the right amount of instincts and intelligence to be able to survive and evolve in the environment in which they find themselves and that in the case of Mankind, he has added the gift of being able to reason so that, increasingly, the awareness of the human race regarding the wonders of creation that are all around for all to see will ensure its ever-increasing knowledge which will, in turn, ensure its eternal progress.

Finally, I would like to comment on the false claim that the Bible is in any way a revelation of God's word. It is, I suggest, nothing more than a collection of books which are of uncertain origin and authorship. The evidence for doubt as to their authenticity is contained in the very books themselves. There are many inaccuracies which any reasonable study of them will reveal. The fact that they have been handed down to us over a vast period of time is not evidence or proof of their authenticity.

I have already explained the vulnerability that the written word is subjected to in the paragraphs above, yet we are expected to take the contents of the Bible and other religious books on trust. In other words, to have blind faith that they are a true record of events as described therein and have not been subject to wrong translation (deliberate or otherwise) or revised without authority etc.

It is a matter of historical fact that the Emperor Constantine of Rome, some three hundred years after the early Christian Church began, set up the Council of Nicea with strict instructions that the row between the two main groups of protagonists within Christianity regarding whether or not The Holy Trinity should be included as part of its doctrine must be resolved without further delay by organising a vote to decide the matter. But even more importantly, he also commanded that they must also vote on which books are in future to be considered the authentic ones that are worthy of inclusion in the Bible and to remove those that they decide are not worthy of inclusion.

As a result of long and heated discussions by the two interested organisations, a vote was taken and it was agreed that The Holy Trinity would be accepted but many books were removed. Many of the priests who were not in favour of this decision and vowed to continue to oppose it as a result were put to death. Emperor Constantine declared that from then on that the Christian religion would be officially recognised as the church of the state of Rome. He now became not only the Emperor of Rome but also the head of the Catholic Church.

Had the outcome of the vote at Nicea resulted in favour of the opposing group of priests the Christian Bible would have contained different books to the existing ones and The Holy Trinity would not have been included. It would automatically follow that all Christians from that moment on would have been obliged to have a different form of faith to that which they have today. This obligation was imposed as a result of the deliberations of self-interested fallible human beings and can in no way be considered as an instruction from God.

In addition to the Bible's origin being unsatisfactory, it is made even more unacceptable in being presented to us as the Word of God by the fact that over the years the original words contained in the Bible have been interpreted and translated in different ways to suit the purposes of various monarchs and different sects of Christianity throughout the world.

Here are just two examples of the many versions that exist throughout the world: There is the King James Bible in the UK. In the USA it was amended to become the American Standard Version Bible. There are, of course, also other versions in a variety of languages in existence throughout Christianity.

Each one of the different versions of the Bible mentioned above have been altered to some degree to suit the purposes of the denomination that has adopted it to satisfy and promote their particular requirements.

I think these are good examples of how the written word is open to corruption and manipulation to suit the purposes of unscrupulous interested parties.

It is an undeniable fact that there cannot be different versions of the truth. The truth is the truth and is not open to interpretation. Either something is the truth or it is not. There is no half way.

CHAPTER TWO

In the previous chapter, I hope I made it clear how it was that I had by now changed from being an agnostic in my religious outlook to that of becoming a Deist. More importantly, I hope, that I have been able to show the inadequacy of the written word to express the wonders of God's creation. As for the written word being chosen by God as the method by which he speaks to us, I say this:

One has only to read the history of what took place at the Council of Nicea, as outlined in the last chapter, to see that the Bible that was put together at that council was the product of fallible human beings within the church hierarchy in direct response to a command from the corrupt Emperor Constantine. It cannot, therefore, be considered as the word of God.

If you accept as I do that God is *perfection*, it is perfectly logical that He would choose a much more reliable and effective way to communicate the *truth* of His existence to Mankind. Although I have outlined my case for this towards the end of the previous chapter, I think it is worth repeating that I believe that the best way for spiritual enlightenment to be achieved is by applying our God-given ability of reason to the perfection that is to be found in the wonderful natural law of creation. By so doing, in the fullness of time we will come to understand more of His wonderful natural laws. He gave us all the gift of being able to *reason* so that each of us can use it to expand our knowledge in our own personal way that is based on conclusions arrived at by logical evaluation and not by having to rely on hearsay from other people.

You can, I hope, see from what I have related to you so far that my wife and I were, at that time, of differing opinions when it came to the question of religion. We had many a discussion on the subject and both put forward our respective views with some passion. However, as neither of us was convinced by our different point of view, we agreed to disagree and left it at that. As it turned out we were soon confronted with a far more urgent challenge which concerned the survival or otherwise of our newly-born son, Michael, the details of which I have already mentioned on page twelve.

It wasn't long after the arrival of Michael that we had the opportunity to move to Luton in Bedfordshire. The offer to move came about as a result of the GLC council house overspill scheme.

The scheme was to enable families, subject to certain criteria being satisfied, being assisted to move to one of the recently developed new towns. These towns were given a sum of money for each family housed and the cost of the construction of the brand new estates was a joint arrangement between the Government and the Greater London Council along with those town councils that were involved in the scheme.

Our family circumstances were such that we qualified to be included in the scheme. We applied and were accepted and in due course we were allocated, a brand new, three-bedroom council house on Lewsey Farm Estate in Luton, Bedfordshire.

However, one of the requirements for us to be able make the move was that I had to be employed within the borough of Luton. This was not a problem for me as I was employed at the time of my application by London Transport as a bus driver at Merton Bus Garage. It was easy for me to arrange a transfer to London Transport Country Bus Garage in Luton. This I did, of course, but as our allocated house was not yet ready for occupation, I had to spend some eleven weeks in lodgings in Luton. I was only able to see my family (who were still in Tooting) on my rest days.

We eventually moved to our new home and in spite of having some regret that we had moved a considerable distance from our relatives, we settled in and soon adapted to our new environment.

It was lovely, of course, to move into a modern, three-bedroom house that had an inside bathroom and separate toilet which, of course, was unlike our flat in Tooting where we had to brave the elements to use the outside lavatory. Of course, it was also great to leave behind the old galvanised bath- tub hanging on the wall in our Tooting flat when we left.

We lived in Luton for about four years during which time we were blessed with another addition to our family. It turned out to be another son and we named him David. Of course, we were thrilled when he arrived but it had been a surprise to us some nine months earlier on being informed by our doctor that Dee was expecting our fourth child, because we had not planned to have any further children.

He was born in the Luton and Dunstable Hospital on the 7th of September 1966. That was the year that England won the World Cup (which David often tells people when he is asked his date of birth). He loves football and is an ardent Luton Town supporter.

We were all quite happy in Luton and so neither Dee nor myself had any intention of moving and if it wasn't for an impending change in my employment situation we probably would not have done so.

The reason we did move came about because of a change of ownership of London Transport Country Buses that was soon to take effect. The government of the day had recently brought in a new transport bill to deregulate the bus operations throughout the land and one of the directives was to split up London Transport into its component parts. The new Transport for London Authority would no longer include London Transport Country Buses as part of its responsibilities.

This coming change would, I considered, affect myself and my family because I would no longer be employed by London Transport and as a result would not continue to receive the better pay and conditions that, at that moment in time, I was receiving. There was also my pension prospects to consider, In addition to this, I said to my wife: "I predict that London Country Buses will be sold off bit by bit to other bus operators and one of the first things to happen will be the closure of Luton LT garage." In due course I was proved to be correct in my prediction.

Fortunately, we by then had successfully managed to arrange a council house exchange to Aveley in Essex and I was able to continue working for London Transport because, although our new home was just outside the London Transport Central Bus operational area, their nearest garage was at that time in Hornchurch, which was in easy reach of it. However, I was informed by LT that I would be unable to take up my duties at Hornchurch immediately on completing my move because of staffing requirements at the garage and would be required to work at Barking garage for about six months.

This did not deter us from moving and after about six months of delay, which was caused by the paperwork of the three councils involved in arranging the move, we were able to move as planned.

We had been trying to arrange a council house exchange for some months prior to this without success. It had proved very difficult for a number of reasons, all beyond our control. We were beginning to become desperate so when we at last had a chance to achieve our goal by accepting a three-way exchange to a place called Aveley, which we hadn't even heard of at that moment in time, we gratefully accepted it.

In hindsight, I think we were meant to move to Aveley because of the events that have taken place since we moved there. I am particularly referring to the fact that of all the neighbours we could have moved to live next door to we found ourselves next door to Bill and Iris Green. They were some time later indirectly responsible for Dee and myself starting our investigation into Spiritualism.

I will describe in the following chapter how this came about. It is my belief that nothing happens just by chance or coincidence and that instead we are all given opportunities to make choices regarding the things that we experience in our lives. The next chapter is, I believe, a good example of this.

CHAPTER THREE

On the day of the move to Aveley, we arrived much later than planned; it was at about six o'clock in the evening on a cold grey February day in 1968. The late arrival was caused by a very late departure from Luton, which was caused by staff difficulties of the removal company we had engaged to carry out the move. The van should have arrived at our house in Luton at 8am. By midday it finally arrived to start the task and this was only because I had telephoned the office at about 10 o'clock to ask why it had not arrived. In answer to my call, I was told by the manager of the office that the team that had been allocated to do the work had not turned up for work that morning and as a result they could not move us that day.

I told him that not only was this unacceptable because he was legally required to carry out a binding contract that had been agreed between us but that, in addition, there would be further difficulties for him because the family who are expecting to occupy our home were at that very moment on the way from London and were due to arrive at any minute.

After a short pause he came back on the line and said that he had been able to find alternative staff and that he personally would be part of the team that will move us as he had already arranged to do.

There were other things that happened on the day of the move but there is no need to relate them here, but suffice to say that our first day in the county of Essex was proving to be very traumatic. (It is little wonder that social scientists say that moving home is rated second only to bereavement with regards to stressful experiences in life).

About two months later, with the arrival of Spring, we all felt better and began to adjust to our new surroundings. The children had settled into their new school without too much difficulty and of course soon made new friends. My wife was also feeling better about the move as well because her mother was able to visit us more easily owing to the fact that her journey from her flat in Balham to our new home in Aveley had been halved.

From here on in we just got on with family life, as any other family does. We experienced the normal ups and downs of life and there is nothing to report of anything outstanding happening in our lives at that moment in time.

Some months later, however, there was an experience that my wife had in a neighbour's house that triggered a change in both of our lives regarding our spiritual beliefs.

As I have previously related to you, Dee and I did not share the same opinion when it came to spiritual matters and we had agreed to let matters of religion remain as they were between us. The result was that we had not discussed the subject since leaving our flat in Tooting. This was to change as a result of the visit by Dee to our neighbours Bill and Iris Green, who lived in the house next door to us.

Whilst she was there, they were engaged in an attempt to contact people who had died and passed on to the Spirit World. They were using a method known as the glass and alphabet system. This consists of arranging the letters of the alphabet in a circle surrounding a tumbler placed in the middle of a table. At the top of the circle the word *yes* is placed and at the bottom of the circle the word *no* is placed. The purpose of this arrangement is to enable the spirit people to be able to spell out, in word form, the details that they wish to communicate. This is hopefully achieved by those taking part placing one finger each on the upturned glass. This action completes the connection of those in the Spirit World with those seated around the table.

However, I wish to point out, that although this method of communication can and does work quite well, it is not recommended that it should be used without first saying an appropriate prayer to God, asking for protection from those in the world of Spirit who have less than good intentions towards those who are present.

Dee had no knowledge at the time of this precaution and in any case she was only an observer of what Bill and Iris were engaged in.

On returning to our house, she told me of the experience she had just witnessed. She said that there was obviously something being achieved on the table but was not happy to just leave it at that.

She said that the thing she had just witnessed had jogged her memory of events that took place back in her childhood when living with her parents in Balham.

Dee said she remembered that an aunt used to visit her mother and tell her of certain things she had seen and heard at Hamilton Hall Spiritualist Church in Balham High Road. She was too young at the time to remember what her aunt had said but the memory also reminded her of an out-of-body experience she herself had whilst she was taking a bath one Sunday morning. She related what happened to her to me saying that whilst relaxing in the lovely hot water, she was suddenly aware that she was looking down at her own back garden and could see her neighbours in their own garden who were enjoying the sunny day. Suddenly, the thought came to her: "Oh, I shouldn't be out here" and as she said this to herself she experienced a sudden jolt and found herself back in her body, immersed in the soothing hot water of her bath.

On hearing this I said to her: "Are you sure that you hadn't momentarily dozed off?" She said: "Yes, I'm sure I didn't because I was not in the bath long enough to dose, and on coming out of the bath; I went straight to the back window that overlooks the gardens." Her neighbours were still out in their garden, just as she had seen them, a few minutes earlier.

On hearing her account I said to her: "You have just reminded me of what I read in that book that my brother Geoff gave me called 'The Masters of The Far East'. It related several cases of out-of-body experiences, in fact it was witnessed by the author that The Masters were able leave their body and travel to other locations at will." This is known as astral travelling.

Dee said that she would like to find out where the nearest Spiritualist church was because she wanted to find out more. I said: "Well, I'm sure Bill will either know or find out for you because he's a postman and when he does find out where it is I would like to come along with you."

Very soon after, Bill did find out for us where the nearest church was and at the same time told us of an extra Saturday meeting that was to take place very soon. He said that he and Iris would like to come along with Dee and I and asked if it would be possible for

Sharon, the girlfriend of one of their sons, to come with the four of us. She was only about sixteen and was temporarily staying with them because both her parents had recently died in fairly quick succession and neither her sister or her brother felt able to offer her a home. And as a result of her situation and her tender years, she was experiencing considerable depression.

I was about to say no, because my small car had only four seats and as Dee was a non-driver at that time she could not act as driver in place of me and so there would not be room for her in the car, when Dee interrupted me and said: "Let her take my place, because now we know where the church is we can go any time we like." This was typical of Dee's generous nature and her kind offer was accepted.

On the Saturday, we arrived to a packed meeting and I had to sit separately from them, but this did not stop us all looking forward to the coming evening, which was a first-time experience for each one of us.

The meeting was hosted by Don Hatch, acting on behalf of the Grays Spiritualist Centre. The guest medium was Gaye Muir, a very experienced medium. After a brief introduction by the president of the centre, she began her demonstration of clairvoyance. This consisted of her being guided by her spirit helper to select individuals seated in the audience for whom there was a message.

Before I continue, I think it may be of help to those of you, who are unfamiliar with mediums working in public to know that the messages are usually fairly brief at public meetings. This is because of the large number of people who are waiting in the audience, who hope to be selected to receive a message. These communications are from anyone on the other side of life who has a purpose in contacting the person to whom the medium has been guided.

The messages can be from anyone that the communicator of the message knew when they were here on the Earth. They are more often than not a relative but they can also be just a friend or an acquaintance of some kind who just wants to let them know that there is no death and that they are very much alive and getting on with this new phase of their life.

I will explain in more detail the way in which mediumship works later on in the book. For the present, however, I hope I have been able to set the scene of our first visit to a Spiritualist meeting.

The medium delivered several messages to people over a wide area of the hall and they were received with a positive response. Then, to my utter astonishment, she selected Sharon, the young girl who was sitting with Bill and Iris and was their lodger at that moment in time. You will remember I told you of how she had asked to come with them to the meeting. I am sure her request to accompany them was as a result of her recent bereavement, coupled with rejection by her brother and sister.

I am going to give the details of the message that she received because of the long-term effects it had, not only to her but also to Bill and Iris and myself and also in due course to my wife, Dee, when she was told of the communication received by Sharon.

Gaye Muir pointed to her saying: "I want to come to the young lady near the back of the hall" and on seeing her startled response, she said: "Don't look behind you, I do mean you." She then went on to give her the following message:

"I have your grandfather here and he is telling me that you thought you saw him standing at the foot of your bed a few weeks ago, is this correct? She answered yes that's right I did. Well he is telling me that you are right he was there, and he says that he is attempting to contact you because he is very concerned at the state of your mind at present. He says you must try and stop thinking in the way you were recently thinking and look forward to the future. You have got a long life ahead of you and you must be positive. He sends his love to you."

I cannot remember the rest of the message, but it was not very much longer and I have related the most important part.

After a few more messages to other people, who all seemed to be satisfied with what had been communicated to them, the meeting came to a close to loud applause.

You can imagine the atmosphere in the car on the journey home was electric because none of us had expected to receive a message on our very first visit to a Spiritualist meeting.

Sharon was fairly quiet on the way home and on arrival at their house, Bill and Iris were told by her the significance of the message that she had received from her granddad. On hearing what she told them, they understood immediately why she had been so subdued in the car on the way home from the meeting. It was because of the accuracy of the communication she had just received.

A day or so after the meeting, Iris told Dee in confidence the real meaning of the grandfathers message to his granddaughter. It was this, that unknown to Bill and Iris, poor Sharon, their lodger, had been contemplating suicide and of course she had not told anyone of her intention and was shocked, to put it mildly, to receive the message from her granddad telling her that he was aware of what she had been thinking.

In time, when she had recovered from the experience, she was able to take great comfort from the knowledge that her granddad was still alive and was able to let her know of his continuing love for her.

I can say that it was from the events that we all witnessed that evening at our first meeting that the resolve of Dee and I to find out more about Spiritualism was strengthened, but more important than this was the effect that the message had on young Sharon, for it proved to be the beginning of her being able to come to terms with the situation she was experiencing at that moment in time and from then on she was able to face her future with more confidence.

Not long after our visit to the meeting outlined above, Sharon's relationship with Graham (the son of Bill and Iris) came to an end, as teenage friendships do and so it was not long before she moved out of their family home. What is so remarkable is that it hadn't been that long ago that Sharon had arrived in a state of considerable depression and yet was now able to move on with her life. This, I am sure, was because of the message she had received from her granddad from the Spirit World. It literally was the start of her being able to change her life around.

This is a classic example of how our loved ones still take a great interest in us even though they have passed on to the next stage of life. It further shows that if the opportunity is presented to them that they can and do get in touch with their loved ones who are still on the Earth plane.

The operative word in the paragraph above is *opportunity*. The vast majority of people are unaware that their deceased loved ones and friends are still alive and getting on with their lives in the realms of Spirit. This can be because of religious reasons (many religions forbid any attempt to contact to the Spirit World) or they may be convinced atheists or agnostics. Of course, it could be that they are just unaware that life goes on and as a result never go to a Spiritualist church or have a private one-to-one sitting with a medium. The result is that anyone on the other side of life who would like to contact them is unable to do so because of the lack of opportunity.

I am sure you will see the logic of this if we just consider the events that I outlined above in the Grays Spiritualist Centre that Saturday evening. I suggest that *just by turning up* at the meeting, Sharon was able to receive that very important message from her ever loving grandfather.

I wonder, if she had not been able to attend that evening, whether she would still be suffering the deep depression she had been suffering for several weeks, or even worse, whether she would have succumbed to her thoughts of suicide .We can never know, of course, but I feel that we must thank God that we were able to take Sharon along to the meeting that turned out to be such a life-changing event for her.

Having experienced the above set of circumstances, both Dee and myself were by now all set to apply ourselves, to finding out more about Spiritualism and so we began to attend the Grays Spiritualist Centre.

This wasn't to be every week because I was a bus driver still and my shift work sometimes prevented us going together. But we were able to attend separately and gradually we both developed each in our own way an understanding of the many facets of Spiritualism.

My first visit to the Grays centre had been to an extra meeting that had been restricted to a demonstration of clairvoyance, which I have already given details of.

My second visit, accompanied by Dee, was to one of the regularly held church services that take place each Sunday and the first thing that impressed and pleased us was the lack of ritual in the service, which had the effect of making us both feel more at ease and welcome.

Of course, although the service was more informal in its approach, there was none the less a proper order of service. This consisted of a greeting and a few words of welcome from the person conducting the service. This was followed by a short period of silence of about three minutes to enable each member of the congregation to send out their own personal thoughts and prayers for those in need. Then came the first hymn, which was followed by a talk chosen by the guest medium, then a second hymn, after which the guest medium's demonstration (usually clairvoyance) was given, followed by a final hymn. Notices of future meetings and guests would bring the service to a close.

The above description is a typical example of the Spiritualist services that are held all over the country, both here and abroad, usually on Sundays.

Dee and I gradually learned the Spiritualist philosophy and witnessed many communications said to be from those on the other side of the veil. The people who received these messages seemed to be in the main satisfied that what they had received was genuine and in time, as we witnessed more and more of this type of communication at further meetings, we too were able to accept that what we had seen and witnessed for ourselves was indeed genuine communication.

CHAPTER FOUR

We both continued on our journey of discovery together whenever that was possible, but also separately. In due course we both began to have the satisfaction of receiving our own messages from our loved ones and friends from the other world.

One fact that we both found surprising is that Spiritualism is one of only two religions in this country to have parliamentary approval. The other one is the Church of England, which is not surprising when you consider the fact that the Church of England has long been recognised as being the religion of the UK and - moreover - its head is none other than the reigning monarch. All other religions are allowed to practice by "Let and Favour only".

In the same way that Christianity embraces many different versions of its beliefs throughout the world, the Spiritualist religion has also, over the course of time, developed several different ways of interpreting the generally accepted Spiritualist philosophy.

The important thing here is, I think, for all the different churches and factions contained within both of the religions mentioned above to first of all recognise the right of others to exist, but also to acknowledge that they each have the right to have a different interpretation with regards to their shared basic beliefs. Secondly - and more importantly - they should concentrate on what they have in common and not on the details of where they differ.

These two principles should apply to all religions throughout the world because if you think about it and simply apply logic to the beliefs of all religions it is reasonable to suggest that the outcome must be that harmony will be achieved. Allow to me point out the main reason for my conclusion: I do not know of any religion that is not based on goodwill toward Mankind. It is because this basic fact has been ignored throughout history that Mankind has been torn apart by intolerance and war.

This truth applies to theology, religion and politics alike and it's inevitable that anywhere in the world where there is one organisation that has the audacity to think that their way is the only way and subsequently goes on to try and enforce their beliefs on others will only create strife and resentment to all concerned, which all too often in the past has eventually led to war.

The thoughts that I have outlined above have been part of the way I have thought for many years. I am first and foremost a democrat and cannot bear to witness intolerance in any field of activities, but especially in the case of religion and politics.

In view of this you, will I'm sure understand how pleased both Dee and I were to find, as our investigations into Spiritualism progressed, that *ritual* and *dogma* has very little part to play in its beliefs or proceedings. Furthermore that each church is run by its own members irrespective of the particular Spiritualist organisation it is affiliated to.

The next thing we found very pleasing is that Spiritualist churches are there to serve everyone, without exception. Anyone of any religious faith, or none, is welcome to take part in the service.

Speaking for myself, I am particularly impressed with the atmosphere that is created in Spiritualist churches. In general they are places where the services are conducted with due reverence to God but are not without humour and also the language used is of the present day. I have never been happy at the way in which out-of-date words (yes, I do mean Latin) are used in some orthodox religious services because, to my way of thinking, it is not only less effective to use a language that the majority of people who are being addressed can't understand but, moreover, it is also disrespectful to the congregation being addressed.

Dee and I continued on our journey of discovery, not only by attending the centre in Grays but also by going to other Spiritualist churches and organisations. In addition to these visits, we began reading some of the many books written on the subject of Spiritualist philosophy.

As time went by, the results of our endeavours secured a gradual change in both of us with regards, to our religious beliefs. In Dee's case, she had found the religious faith she had been seeking for so many years. I, for my part, could also feel that I could from now on embrace the teachings and philosophy of Spiritualism.

We both enrolled as members of the Grays Spiritualist Centre and continued on our journey of spiritual enlightenment.

As I pointed out in the preface to this book, I have never been a person to keep good written records of dates and events that I have experienced throughout my life. I accept that I have been negligent and it is my intention, therefore, for the rest of this book to try and compensate for the absence of dates. I will do this by relating each event in as much detail as I can. In addition to this, when I am giving an account of spirit messages and events we have witnessed, I will attempt to explain why the communication can be considered to be good evidence or otherwise.

By doing this, I will be concentrating on the contents and evidence of the communications which is, in most cases, far more important than the date upon which the event took place.

I wish to emphasise at this point that the experiences that I will be relating to you in this book are similar to the thousands of messages that have been received by countless numbers of people throughout history.

As you read of my experiences, it is important for you to judge for yourself what credence you give to them. I ask only that you apply reason and logic to what I have to say. If, after due consideration, you find it offends your own sense of reason, I suggest only then that it is reasonable for you to reject it.

The principle of reason being applied to the evidence for survival of physical death is the very basis on which the Spiritualist religion is founded. Unlike other religions, it offers evidence to prove survival after death and does not expect you to rely solely on blind faith. Further to this, Spiritualism does not suggest that its beliefs are the only way to find God. Neither does it say that for you to believe anything other than that which is being presented to you is to condemn yourself to some sort of eternal punishment. On the contrary, one of the basic principles of Spiritualist philosophy is *that all persons irrespective of their faith survive physical death*.

It may be helpful for me at this point to list the generally accepted Seven Principles of Spiritualism:

1 The Fatherhood of God
2 The Brotherhood of Man
3 Communion of Spirits and the Ministry of Angels

4 The continuous existence of the human Soul
5 Personal Responsibility
6 Compensation and Retribution hereafter for all good and evil deeds done on Earth
7 Eternal Progress open to every human Soul

I cannot see anything in the above Seven Principles that can offend any fair-minded person. I found principle number five particularly appealing when I first became acquainted with the list because it is, I believe, always the case that you should take responsibility for your actions and it is totally wrong to think *that anyone other than the person who carried out the action* can take either the credit or the blame for the resulting consequences of their actions.

The above list of the Seven Principles was compiled by the Spiritualist National Union in the year 1890 as a result of the communications that were received from the realms of Spirit. The Seven Principles are a good example of principle number three, as listed above, being used with great effect and is in accord with the other six principles.

Most of the other Spiritualist organisations have been happy to adopt the list; in most cases without any modification. I think this is because if any one of the principles is considered separately, it can be seen to be absolutely compatible with the other six principles.

Dee and I continued to attend the Grays centre and also other Spiritualist churches that were in easy reach of where we lived. We, in addition to this, continued to increase our knowledge and understanding of Spiritualism by reading some of the many books on the subject, some of which were written by famous people who are well known for their work in other spheres. One of these books was by the late Sir Arthur Conan Doyle. His books, even to this day, are as popular as ever a writer of mystery and intrigue could be. He possessed, as one book reviewer stated, "a brilliant and deductive mind, one that was razor-sharp."

He used his wonderful gift of reasoning, that he had used so many times, to write enthralling mystery detective adventures. He probed the subject of Spiritualism and resulting from this dedicated work, his book entitled 'The History Of Spiritualism', which consisted of two volumes, was published. He had observed that, although there had been many books written on the subject of Spiritualism, there had not as yet been, at that time, one that could be described as a *history of the subject* and so he set about the task of putting that to rights. He did so with great application and skill.

As a result of the knowledge he had gained since he first became a convinced Spiritualist, he dedicated the rest of his life to propagating its philosophy throughout the world.

My wife and I were very fortunate to have found the Grays Spiritualist Centre, in particular, because, on becoming members, we were able to loan books from its well-stocked library. Some of the books were no longer in print. This meant, of course, that the knowledge we gained was more comprehensive than it otherwise would have been and this in turn helped us to arrive at an even fuller understanding of the Spiritualist religion.

It was through my own personal investigation into Spiritualism that I found that my Deist belief was not compromised in any way by the philosophy of Spiritualism; in fact, if anything, it is enhanced. I am also pleased that the theory of evolution by Charles Darwin is accepted by most Spiritualists without any problem.

There are many people who state that Darwin's famous theory is very comprehensive and that it proves that there is no God. They arrive at their conclusion by combining the evidence shown by geologists with that of Darwin to show that the world was not created in six days but took millions of years to evolve.

Whilst it is a fact that Darwin's evidence, together with that of geologists, is without any doubt ample proof of evolution, it cannot, in addition, be shown to prove that God does not exist. Neither can it be said of the early theologians that, just because they got their facts wrong concerning creation having been achieved in six days, it does not follow that they were, therefore, wrong to believe in the existence of God.

Spiritualist philosophy is able to add another dimension to the understanding of evolution by its explanation that, in addition to the known structures that are present in all the atoms throughout the cosmos, there is, the additional presence of the Great Spirit, which is the natural law that is responsible for all of creation. This natural law is God. It is this spiritual presence that determines the progress and development of matter throughout the universe by the Law of Cause and Effect.

Everything that exists in the cosmos is governed by the natural law that is God, the Great Spirit. It is Spirit that controls matter, not the other way round.

Many people say that they cannot believe in the existence of God because they cannot see him. Yet those same people are quite happy to believe in other things that can't be seen with their normal five senses. I am thinking here of such things as TV signals, X-rays, Radio Waves, Electricity etc. It is a fact that all of these can only be seen to exist by having the right equipment to convert the wavelengths of the forces involved to become visible to the limitations of our five senses. It is also a fact that we can all have knowledge of the existence of other locations and towns and planets etc, without having personally been there. This is because in all the above examples there is ample evidence that is freely available to everyone to offer the proof of their existence.

It is not unreasonable for anyone to require proof of the evidence being offered to them on any given subject and I have already given my reasons why I am happy to believe in the existence of a supreme being earlier on in this book. To avoid repetition, I refer you to chapter one, pages 12, 13 and 14.

Science has proven that everything in our world, whether it be animal, mineral, or vegetable, consists of atoms and that every atom has a nucleus around which there are protons and neutrons circulating in much the same way that our Earth, together with the other planets, travels around the sun.

Scientists working in many different fields of study have all found that, throughout the cosmos, from the smallest particles known to the largest they are all subject to the Law of Cause and Effect. They have also found that, the more they have discovered, there is even more that is yet to be discovered about the natural laws of creation.

Of course the scientific study of the cosmos is obviously ongoing and is a vast undertaking and I am not equipped to elaborate any further on the subject. Even if I had the skill and knowledge to do so, it is not the purpose of this book to pursue the subject further.

However, before I leave the subject of the evolving universe to return to the original purpose of my book, I would like to make it clear that all the scientific knowledge and information I have learned has not in any way affected my belief in Spiritualism, because I know that, generally speaking, science is only concerned with things that consist of matter. This means that the spiritual dimension is not usually taken into consideration.

CHAPTER FIVE

Most people who attend Spiritualist churches for the first time soon become aware of the main differences in the way the service and worship is conducted.

In orthodox Christian churches of any denomination the focus of the service is around the minister, who conducts the service in accordance with the laid down format of the particular faith that they represent. It usually consists of hymns and set prayers, which are usually preordained by the hierarchy of the particular faith that the church represents. In addition to the prayers and hymns, the vicar will give a sermon and also a reading from the Bible and as a matter of course, The Lord's Prayer.

The words that the vicar chooses to use in his sermon can be of his own choosing but the theme is usually found to be in sympathy with the particular interpretation of the faith to which he belongs.

The worship and contents of most Spiritualist church services are considerably different. Earlier on in the book, I outlined the fact that most Spiritualist churches are run by its members. This means that they are able to decide on the order and contents of the service to a much greater degree. Often The Lord's Prayer can be part of the proceedings because its words are very much accepted by most people, whatever their own personal beliefs or religion happens to be.

The service is opened and conducted by the president, or chairperson, who's job it is to introduce and welcome the guest medium. The medium is the main contributor to the service and usually opens with a prayer that is chosen by them. This is then usually followed by a talk (often referred to as an 'Address'). After a hymn the medium is then free to communicate with our friends in Spirit on behalf of those gathered together with the blessing of God. After completing the messages, the medium or the president then closes the meeting in prayer.

The order of service at the Grays Spiritualist Centre is conducted very much as outlined above and as I have already told you, it was there that our early years of learning about Spiritualism took place.

As time went by, we also experienced other events at other locations, which added to our knowledge and of course our book reading was also a very important aid to this joint endeavour. In addition to our many attendances at the various places connected with Spiritualism, there was one very important spiritual communication that we received in our own home, which turned out to be not only very good evidence for life after death but, in due course, turned out to be of great help to Connie, who was one of my sisters.

I am going to relate to you in great detail both how the message from Spirit was received and how it proved to be so very helpful, not only to Connie but also to her family. On reading what follows, I hope you will be able to see just how valuable good spiritual communication can be.

You will recall how Dee had seen the glass and alphabet being used to contact Spirit in our neighbour's house soon after our move to Aveley.

This was the first thing that had influenced her to want to find out where the nearest Spiritualist church was and I have already told you earlier in the book of how Bill, our neighbour, found out for her and also of the first attendance there by Bill, Iris, Sharon and myself, which resulted in Dee and myself becoming involved with Spiritualism.

We had learnt from our studies into Spiritualism, that one of the ways of achieving contact with our friends, guides and helpers in the Spirit World is by the use of the glass and alphabet system, as previously described. We were aware that it must only be used sensibly and with a prayer to God, asking for protection from those people in the realms of Spirit, who do not come with love and understanding. Furthermore, I want to make clear that the use of the glass and alphabet method is a poor substitute for contacting Spirit when compared to the help of a competent medium.

We knew this, of course, but decided one evening that we would to try the method for ourselves, so, together with our daughter, Deena, we set out the letters of the alphabet and the words *yes* at the top and *no* at the bottom. We placed a small upturned glass in the centre of the circle of letters. I said a suitable prayer and then we each placed a finger lightly on the glass.

Within a very short space of time the glass seemed to become energised because it started to spell out the names of every one of my brothers and sisters. We asked who the communicator was and the glass moved to spell out the word "mum". At that moment we realised it must be my mother who was in communication with us because Dee's mother was still alive on the Earth plane.

The glass then went on to spell out the following message. It took the form of a request to us, as follows: "tell Connie not to keeping shouting at Robert." After expressing her love and saying "good- bye," the message ended. We were aware of this because the glass was no longer energised and remained motionless. We were satisfied after waiting for several minutes that there was not going to be any further communication and so I closed the session with a prayer.

We then considered what we had just received. Of course, all the names we had been given were familiar to all three of us, so we reasoned as follows: Could it be that as all the names were in each of our memories, we might have unintentionally moved the glass ourselves to make up the list of our relatives' names. On reflection, we decided that this was highly unlikely because we would all have had to think of them in the same sequence. Further to this, there was the short message to be taken into account. None of us understood what the message meant and also it was entirely unlikely that all three of us would come up with the same choice of words and so we, therefore, agreed that it was more likely that the message had indeed been a genuine communication from my mother.

My sister, Connie, at that moment in time, was living with her husband and their three children in Bristol and we had not heard from them for over two years so there was no way that we could know what the contents of the message referred to.

We decided that it was not the sort of thing that we could ask Connie about, not least because of the nature of the communication. It was, we thought, of a rather personal nature and that Connie might not be very pleased that we had knowledge of the situation prevailing in her family at that moment in time. She could be very upset by hearing from us that we had such knowledge of whatever the message was referring to and so we decided that we would not contact her. However, it was some weeks later as a result of a visit we made to another sister that our decision took on a new dimension.

We went on a visit to my sister, Dorothy, who was living in Epsom in Surrey. During the visit she asked us if we were still looking into Spiritualism and if so what was the latest we had to tell her. Of course, we replied in the affirmative and I told her in great detail about the message we had received from our mother. She reacted with the expression: "Good God!" and went on to ask: "Have you told Connie about it?" To which I replied: "No" and gave her the reasons why I hadn't as I have already outlined above.

Dorothy said: "Well, if you both have no objection, I am going to tell her about the message you received because it is possibly just what Connie needs just now." She went on to tell us that Connie and her husband, Jack, were both having difficulty with regards to their relationship with their teenage son, Robert. His name was mentioned in the message, you will remember. Apparently, he was very undecided about what he wanted to do regarding his future. This was causing considerable disruption within the family and Connie, who I am afraid had a very short temper, was having terrible rows with him. Connie had a blood pressure condition and of course this family concern was adding stress to her health problem.

This was all news to us because we had not been in touch with Connie and Jack for at least two years and so we were completely unaware of anything regarding their present family situation.

We could now understand the message we had received that evening several weeks earlier. It was now obvious to us both that my mother was aware of the conditions existing within Connie's family and wanted to help each of them to overcome the unsatisfactory relationship that was affecting their family at that particular moment in time.

This is a very good example of what I have outlined to you earlier in this book when I told you that it is the most natural thing for parents, who having left the Earth plane, to want to continue to help their loved ones here on Earth in any way they can. I also told you of how they are often unable to do so, owing to the fact that most people on Earth do not visit Spiritualist churches or go to private sittings with good mediums. This means that the opportunity is not available to them to make their presence known to their loved ones.

I think you can now see that my mother was able to set in motion a series of events that would be of benefit to Connie and her family. She was aware that Dee, together with myself and Deena, were planning to use the glass and alphabet to see if we could achieve communication with the world of Spirit.

Here was the opportunity that she was able to use to help Connie and Robert come to together and reach a better understanding, which in turn resolved what was, up to that moment in time, a very trying family situation.

A short time after our visit to Dorothy's, she was true to her word and contacted Connie. She told her of the recent visit she had had from us and also, of course, in great detail, the message we had received from our mother in Spirit.

Connie must have been very impressed with what Dorothy had informed her of because Dorothy let us know some time later that Connie had sat down with her son, Robert and had a heart-to-heart talk with him as a direct result of what she had been told by her sister, Dorothy.

He in turn must have been very moved by the content of the message because gradually he was able to adjust and improve his relationship with his mother and father.

This all happened many years ago and he has proved, with the passage of time, to be a wonderful son and a great brother to both his sister, Gill and his brother, John and is also a loving husband and father too.

I think it would be helpful for me to emphasise some important facts about the above account I have told you before I move on to other events. The first thing to note is that when we sat down in our home that evening to attempt to communicate with Spirit by the use of the glass and alphabet, we had never attempted to do so before and had no idea if we would be successful. Secondly, we had not decided on whom we wished to contact. Thirdly, when we had received the message and were satisfied that it was complete, we closed the session with a thankful prayer.

We knew from our knowledge of Spiritualist teachings that one should never just accept a message as being genuine without first applying certain criteria to test its validity.

Where a medium is being used to communicate any type of message, one should always be satisfied that there is no way that the medium could have any knowledge of the content of the message being given by any other method than that of spiritual communication.

In our attempt at communication in our home that evening there wasn't any medium present and so we questioned the source and authenticity of the message by using our sense of reason. We first of all considered whether it could have been by a subconscious effort by us that caused the glass to move. We decided that the answer was no, because it is highly unlikely that we would all be thinking of the list of relatives we had received at the same time and in the same order. In addition to this, we decided that as all three of us had no idea what the message meant, it could not reasonably be thought to have come from any source other than Spirit because, remember, none of us had had any news concerning Connie and her family for about two years.

I have given a very accurate and detailed account of what took place in our home that evening and also of the visit to my sister Dorothy's home for the following reason: I want readers to be able to judge for themselves whether they consider our conclusion that this was a genuine spiritual communication to be a reasonable assessment.

Proof of any given set of facts relies on the quality of the evidence being offered and I submit that the evidence I have given in great detail satisfies that requirement in every respect.

There was another event that again took place in my sister Dorothy's home when we were on another visit to her. It was quite some time after the visit I have already told you about and it was also as the result of Dorothy asking if we were still pursuing our investigations into Spiritualism. We told her that we were both still involved with increasing our knowledge of the subject of Spiritualism as we both now considered it to be our religion and that Dee was now sitting in a development circle to develop her spiritual gifts. She had been told by several mediums that she had the potential to become a medium herself and had been fortunate to find a development circle that had a vacancy that she was able to fill.

On hearing this, Dorothy wanted to know more about circle work and its purpose so Dee and I did our best to explain to her that the purpose of a circle varies according to the particular spiritual gift that one is seeking to develop. We told her that some circles sit in order to develop clairvoyance or clairaudience. Others sit to develop trance mediumship or the gift of spiritual healing.

All of these gifts are some times referred to as a 'sixth sense' and this is pretty accurate because none of them are physical but are a psychic gift that all people possess to varying degrees. Some people have more of any one gift than do others but this does not preclude anyone from sitting to develop their psychic awareness.

This extra sense can also been seen in the animal kingdom. A good example of this is shown by pigeons with their ability to navigate their way home even when they have been freed in an area completely unknown to them. Another example are the wonderful skills of navigation and timing shown by flocks of birds when they fly distances of thousands of miles each year during migration. Also it has often been reported how dogs and cats have found their way back to their former homes after the family has moved to a new home.

All of the above are examples of an inbuilt sixth sense being used and are a direct result of the evolution of the spirit that is within not only we humans but is also to be found in all creatures on Earth.

In giving further examples of spiritual gifts, I mentioned the gift of psychometry and said that Dee had some experience of being able to use this particular gift. Dorothy asked what it was and I told her it consisted of the sensing of the information that is present in inanimate objects. These can be anything that have been in contact with a human being or have even been present when certain things have taken place. Items of jewellery or other personal items are often the kind of things that are presented for an appraisal.

This consists of the medium holding the item in her hands, usually with eyes closed and with quietness being observed. She will concentrate on the item and if she is aware of anything coming into her mind she will then tell the sitter whatever it is that she is receiving. The best results using this method are often achieved when the item being used is a personal possession that has preferably not been handled or worn by any other person.

On hearing the explanation, Dorothy asked Dee if she would try to give a reading on something she had had in her possession for many years. Dee said she would try but added that she was not very experienced at psychometry and could not promise to be successful. Dorothy replied that she understood and went off to get the item from a nearby sideboard. From an old shoebox, she produced a fountain pen and handed it to Dee and asked if she would try and see if she could get anything from it. Dee replied that she would but cautioned Dorothy to tell her nothing whatsoever about the pen she had just passed to her.

Dee then closed her eyes and held the pen in her hands. We all sat in silence to assist Dee with what she was attempting to achieve. After about two or three minutes, Dee said that she was aware of a great amount of noise around her and then said: "Oh dear, I've just had a very sharp pain on the side of my head." She waited a minute or two and then said: "I am sorry, I am not getting anything more and I don't think I will." After a moment or two more she opened her eyes and said: "I am sorry but that is all I could get."

Dorothy replied: "Don't be sorry, because you cannot know just how accurate the information you have just received is" and went on to tell us why she thought it so evidential. But before I give you the details of what she had to tell us, I wish to stress that none of us had ever met the person who was the owner of the fountain pen and that when Dorothy handed the pen to Dee for her to attempt the reading, she had said nothing about it.

This is what my sister went on to relate to us: The owner of the pen had been a boyfriend of my auntie Ada during the First World War. They were very much in love and intended to become engaged. However, this wasn't to be because he was in the army on active service in France and was killed in action. He had received a bullet wound to his head, which proved fatal.

It was immediately obvious to all three of us that Dee had picked up the conditions present at the time of his death from the fountain pen and that this had proved to be a very good example of just how accurate psychometry can be when given the right conditions.

I had only met my auntie Ada a few times during the Second World War and only once or twice after. I had no knowledge of her personal history. She died in 1963 and my wife, Dee, had never met her. My sister, Dorothy, was considerably older than me so had, of course, met our auntie many times over the years but neither she or any of the other members of my family had ever mentioned the details of our auntie's sad loss. It is more likely that they had no knowledge of the event that had taken place in France.

These two visits to my sister Dorothy's house had turned out to have provided additional proof to both Dee and I that we were treading the path of spiritual enlightenment that was meant for us.

Dee was greatly encouraged by her successful psychometry reading and continued to sit in her development circle in order to develop her gifts. She was hoping in time to become able to use them well enough to be of service to other people.

Unlike Dee, I was unable to sit in a development circle because of my shift work pattern of employment. I was still at this time a bus driver and this meant that I was unable to commit to attending at a regular time each week to any type of circle work. Regular attendance is a requirement of all circle work but this does not preclude one from developing any personal psychic gifts that one has in other ways, as I was to find out in the years to come.

Although it is preferable to be able develop ones psychic gifts within a circle of people with the same goals, it is by no means the case that spiritual development cannot be achieved by individuals, but their commitment to serve must be just as firm as is required by circle membership. This, of course, needs a much higher degree of self-discipline. In addition to this, it is essential to be patient and persistent, whether as a member of a circle or as an individual. This is because there are many things that must be in place on both sides of the veil before the right conditions are created for harmony in working together can be achieved. This harmony is not always achieved easily because it is a fact that good intentions on their own are not enough. There must also be compatibility between the sitters on the Earth side of the circle as regards to what type of spiritual phenomena they are seeking. By this, I mean, are they sitting for trance, physical, clairvoyance or healing? The purpose of the circle vacancy should always be made clear and should also be understood by the person wishing to join the circle.

It is important to remember that the purpose of all circle work is to serve the Great Spirit in co-operation with our spirit guides and helpers. It is also advisable to be aware that the process of developing this co-operation and achieving results can be a long process. Many of the mediums well known for their very considerable ability to deliver accurate evidential messages had to be very patient and sit for a number of years to develop their spiritual gifts.

In the following chapter I will show how some messages received can be life-changing when acted upon. The first message is a good example of this. It concerned me being able to take up spiritual healing if I so desired. The second message I received came some time later. It gave me advanced notice of an opportunity that would soon arise at my place of work regarding my employment prospects that would, if acted upon in a positive way, allow me to expand my healing work.

I, of course, have free will (as indeed we all have) as to whether to make a positive response to opportunities, or ignore them. I am pleased to say that I took the positive option in both of the following cases I am about to relate to you.

Further to what I have already mentioned regarding free will, I would like to make it clear that our friends and loved ones cannot interfere with our choices even though at times they can see that our decisions are not always in our best interests.

This is because the decisions we make in life are part of our learning and spiritual development. Our life on Earth is just part of our eternal journey. We have been told many times from our friends in Spirit that it is when we are facing hardship and finding the way forward difficult to face that it is at those times that we grow in spiritual knowledge. We have also been told that things that are easily achieved are of little value. The things we have to strive for, sometimes under great difficulty, are the things of greatest value to us with regards to our spiritual journey.

Because we cannot see into the future, we have to simply trust our own judgement and it is only in hindsight that we can see whether our decision was for the best or otherwise. This is how it must be or we would never learn by our mistakes. It is why God gave us the ability to reason things out and way up the pros and cons for ourselves when we are confronted with the challenges that we must all face in our lives.

Having made our decision, we must take full responsibility for the outcome. Personal responsibility is, in my view, among the most important of The Seven Principles of Spiritualism because no one should be asked to take the blame for someone else's wrongdoing. Equally, they should not take the credit for the good things that are done by other people.

CHAPTER SIX

Soon after I had accepted the truth of Spiritualist philosophy, I received, on more than one occasion, messages from Spirit by different mediums that I had the potential to become a healer. This really pleased me, not only because I had for some time been attracted to this particular spiritual gift, but also because I had received this information on several different occasions from three or four different mediums. This meant that the message concerning my ability to heal was more likely to be accurate than if I had received the message on only one occasion.

Soon after hearing these messages I decided that I would like to try my hand at healing. This meant that I needed to find a way to develop my gift, but I was not sure how to do so because I was still a bus driver and of course this entailed shift duties. I was, therefore, unable to look for a healing circle to join owing to the fact that I would not be able to commit to regular attendance at the circle each week.

The solution to my dilemma came about sooner than I expected, as a direct result of me mentioning what I had been told in the messages I had received to Dick Eaton. He was one of the healers at the Grays Spiritualist Centre. He was attending my wife to give her healing in our home at the time that I told him about the messages. He suggested that I assist him with the healing of my wife if I so desired. I was more than willing to do as he suggested and within minutes I was helping him to give healing to her.

In addition to his healing gift, Dick was also a clairvoyant and after the healing session was completed, he said he could confirm that I had the potential to be used for healing as he was aware of the presence of my spiritual guide who was assisting us with the healing.

On hearing this, I asked him how I could develop my gift and told him about my shift work, which precluded me from seeking a healing development circle. He said that I could develop my gift by sitting quietly and asking Spirit if I may be allowed to work with them to achieve healing for those in need. He went on to say that

I should not make this request for help in developing my gift without first giving it very serious thought. He went on to say that healing is a great responsibility and requires dedication and morality and trustworthiness. It also requires great commitment, not only to The Great Spirit, but also to the people for whom we are attempting the healing.

I was already aware of these essential requirements and also of the dedication that is required with regards to all spiritual work. I, therefore, set about obtaining as much information as I could in addition to acting on the sound advice that Dick had given me.

I made my first task, that of sitting in meditation, to help develop my gift of healing. I also set about reading as much as I could on the subject, especially the books written by the world renowned healer, Harry Edwards.

Not only has he written many books on the subject of spiritual healing but he also opened the very successful healing sanctuary in the county of Surrey, known as The Harry Edwards Healing Sanctuary. This is a large, wonderfully situated house which stands in its own grounds at Burrows Lea in Shere in Surrey. It is a registered charity and does not charge for its healing services, but will accept donations.

In addition to his work at the sanctuary, where he gave healing alongside his team, he also travelled all over the country to some of the largest halls, including, among others, the Royal Albert Hall in London to give public demonstrations of spiritual healing. He did this right up to his death in 1978.

My wife, Dee and I were able to go to one of his public demonstrations, which took place on the 8th of April 1975 at the Cliffs Pavilion in Southend-on-Sea, Essex. What we both witnessed there was so wonderful that it was one of the events that was instrumental in both of us wanting to develop our respective spiritual gifts further. I cannot recall if it was before or after seeing him work that Dee remembered having met him before. This is what she told me:

Towards the end of the Second World War, she was visiting her dad's parents in Balham, who lived just around the corner from where she lived. It was on a Sunday and she was only about four or five at the time. Her grandfather was in the local Home Guard and used to sometimes bring his officer home for Sunday tea. This officer was none other than Harry Edwards. There is a picture of them sitting together in Harry Edwards' biography, surrounded by the rest of the Balham Home Guard platoon.

A few months after we had attended Harry's healing demonstration at Southend, we went to a psychic film show at the Queen Elizabeth Hall on the South Bank in London on the 28th of October 1975, where I was pleased to be able to reintroduce Dee to Harry. It came about in the foyer. I was waiting for Dee to rejoin me in the foyer after the show when I noticed Harry talking to some people near to where I was standing. Before the commencement of the film, he, together with other people who were well known people in the Spiritualist movement, had been introduced to the audience in the hall.

I took the opportunity to introduce myself to him and then I asked him if he could recall visiting Mr Tyrrell, who was a member of his Home Guard Platoon in Balham during the war. He replied: "Good heavens, yes I do remember" and said: "My word, that was a long time ago." I then asked him if he could recall Mr Tyrrell's little granddaughter, Dorothy, who was often there at the time of his visits. He said he did remember her and was in the middle of asking why I was asking him when he was interrupted by Dee joining us both. I was immediately able to answer his question by introducing her to him as the little girl who he remembered from his days in Balham during the war. I was glad to tell him that I was proud to be her husband.

Unfortunately, circumstances did not permit a long conversation but he did give her a very warm handshake and said how nice it was to meet her again before we went our separate ways. It was a moment we both treasured ever after.

In time I found that my healing gift was developing and that I was getting very good results and this was, I felt sure, because I was co-operating with my guides and helpers to be a good channel for the necessary healing to take place. In addition to this, I was finding that, on offering my services to people in need, most of them were only too willing to give spiritual healing a try. As for those who expressed their doubts regarding whether it would work for them, because they were not of any religious faith, I was able to explain to them that faith was not required.

I explained that animals have received healing many times all over the world and so have infants and babies. None of them are even aware of the healing that is taking place. Healing does not require faith. Spiritual healing is not to be confused with faith healing.

All healing comes from God, whatever we conceive him to be. It is a fact that God loves us all because of who he is, not because of anything we may or may not believe.

I found that as I continued to help people, those who felt that the healing had been of benefit to them wanted to help others to know of the benefits of spiritual healing. I began to be directed by them to other people requiring help with various ailments. This way of working by recommendation suited me very well for several reasons. I was much more comfortable applying healing in a home environment on a one-to-one basis rather than in a church healing session. It also was, in many cases, more acceptable to the patients because it overcame the difficulty for those people who were not happy to attend a church healing service. More importantly, it overcame the problem of those who, although willing to attend, are unable to do so for a variety of different reasons.

In addition to this, I was somewhat hindered in my endeavours by my shift work. I was still a bus driver and I was not always able to be available to give healing on a consistent basis. The need for treatment to be continuous can be quite important for some conditions but less so in others. Spiritual healing is just like orthodox healing methods in that, for some ailments, there is a need for only one or two visits to overcome the condition that the patient is suffering from, but for other types of illness there is a need for a course of treatment on a continuing basis.

You can now see why I was somewhat frustrated in my healing endeavours owing to my shift work as a bus driver. I continued to go about my healing work in spite of this hindrance for some years. Then a change in my employment circumstances came about in a most remarkable way that would in future enable me to work regular hours. This change meant that I could, in future, promise those people who required ongoing healing to have un-interrupted visits from me.

How this change in my working conditions from having to work shift duties to being able to work regular hours is not only interesting because of the way it came about but is also a classic example of how our friends in the Spirit Realms can help us achieve our goals.

I will relate in great detail how my circumstances changed, not only because of the remarkable way it came about, but also because it is the second time that I had been told in advance by spirit friends that I would be able to do my spiritual work of healing more effectively because of coming changes at my place of work.

The above message was received and relayed to me by four different mediums on four different occasions. This, I felt, must mean that a change will happen, but at that point I just could not see how.

One of the mediums also mentioned that she was being shown that at some time in the near future I would be standing in a room surrounded by people who were all of senior management status. This I again could not understand because, as a bus driver, I had no contact with senior management in the course of my normal working day.

I did not give much thought to what I had been told and continued to go about my daily life as usual. This was mainly because I was very contented with my job and Dee was used to my shift duties, as were my children. In addition to this, my income was quite good and being employed by London Transport, I had security and a good pension to look forward to.

In the course of time both the predictions in the above messages came about. The first one to happen was the one concerning me standing in a room and being surrounded by senior management and some time later the other part of the message regarding the change to my working hours.

In both cases, how the events happened to allow the truth of the predictions to be fulfilled is very interesting and so in the next chapter I am going to give a detailed account of how both the predictions contained in the spirit messages came to fruition.

CHAPTER SEVEN

One day on arrival at Hornchurch Bus Garage, I went, as usual, to sign on for my duty for that day and adjacent to the signing on sheet was a note from the garage manager. It requested me to see him before I was due to start my day's work and so I duly went along to his office.

He said he wanted to see me regarding a staff visit and went on to explain to me that every year he was required to nominate any members of his staff that merit being considered for a staff visit under the Lord Ashfield scheme. He said that he intended to submit my name for consideration if I was agreeable.

I asked him for further details of the scheme and he said the scheme was introduced before the War to reward staff in recognition of their service. He went on to explain that the visits varied and some were just a day to be shown around a local company or college but that sometimes the visit could be more elaborate, such as a recent one which was where staff went to the USA to accompany two Route Master buses on a goodwill visit representing London Transport at a trade fair.

He said he had no idea whether I would be successful in being selected or what type of visit it would be. He asked me if I would like to have my name submitted. I replied that I would.

Some weeks later the garage manager called me in again to inform me that I had been successful in being included as one of a party of eight L.T. staff scheduled to visit the town of Bradford in Yorkshire. It would be over a period of four days with all expenses paid, including hotel accommodation.

I was thrilled to have been selected and of course I accepted the offer. I was informed that the visit would consist of visiting various places of interest as follows: The new Bradford Interchange, which was at that time still in the course of construction. It was a fourteen million pound development consisting of a combined bus and coach station built adjacent to the existing rail station. Our host for this part of the trip was Bradford's transport manager.

Over the four days, we went on to visit four other places consisting of a spinning mill, a weaving mill, the GEC's electric motor works and lastly to Bradford's Conditioning Centre, which is where the woollen industry refers all its wool and materials for valuation and quality purposes.

It was on the evening of our final day of visiting all these establishments that London Transport had arranged for all the managers of the firms we had visited to be entertained to a dinner at our hotel to express our thanks and appreciation of the four day visit.

During that evening I suddenly realised that I was standing in a room surrounded by senior management. I next remembered that I had already been told that this would happen some months earlier in one of the messages that I had received from one of my friends in Spirit. At the time of receiving the message I could not see how, as a bus driver, I could possibly be surrounded by management, let alone senior management, because my duties did not entail me being in contact with them.

What I had failed to appreciate was that our friends in Spirit have a foresight with regards to coming events to a certain degree and can inform us of things that are likely to happen. This does not in any way mean that the event will definitely take place because we have free will and in exercising that will we can affect the outcome.

The other prediction that I had received from the four mediums regarding a forthcoming change to my working conditions came about in an even more unexpected way.

I was not actively looking to change my occupation for the very good reasons that I have already told you about. There was no way I could see of achieving regular hours of work and still be employed by L.T. and so it was my intention to continue driving buses for the foreseeable future.

The opportunity for me to effect a change in my working conditions that would enable me to work regular hours came about in a way that I could not have dreamt of. It again started at Hornchurch Bus Garage and yet again it was just as I had signed on for my days work.

Adjacent to the signing-on sheet there was a staff advertisement. It said that there were two vacancies for publicity inspectors in the bus operating section of London Transport's Publicity Department. It gave a description of the duties and hours required together with the location of where the operations were based. It went on to detail the particular type of work involved. I was immediately interested because the work sounded very interesting and the status of inspector meant that I would not lose out financially, plus there was no shift work involved.

I decided to apply for one of the positions even though I realised that the advertisement would have been posted throughout London Transport. I said to my wife that the chances for my being successful were pretty slim but she agreed that the job was well worth trying for. I, therefore, applied for one of the vacancies.

I had noted, when I read the advertisement, that it was only about three days before the closing date for applications to be accepted. This, I thought, could be a problem as there was a national postal strike in force at the time. I remembered, however, that London Transport has its own internal mail system and I was able to use it to beat the deadline.

A week or so later, I was informed by my garage manager that I had been accepted along with some fifty-six other applicants to attend the publicity department for an interview. Well, I was pleased, of course, but I was still aware that my chances of being successful were still pretty long odds (in bookmaker's terms it was 57-1).

I went to Griffith House in London for the interview. When I came out I felt I had done reasonably well. This proved to be the case as a few weeks later I was called to be one of seven applicants to be put on the shortlist.

On attending this final interview, I felt this time it had gone very well for me; in fact, as I was riding on the bus home I suddenly had the thought come to me that my spirit friends had told me quite some time ago *that a change would come in my working conditions and as a result I would be able to carry out my spiritual work more easily.*

It was at that moment that I became almost certain that my interview had been successful and that I would be offered one of the vacancies.

A week or two later my garage manager informed me that I had been successful in my application and gave me the date for my transfer to L.T. Publicity at Walthamstow Bus Garage.

The reader should easily be able to deduce from the facts that I have related above that our spirit friends have a certain amount of knowledge as to coming events in our lives, hence they were able to let me know in advance of the two events that I have described above.

It is important to be aware, however, that, although this is the case, they are not allowed by natural law to interfere with our decisions concerning our affairs, because that would be interfering with our God-given free will.

This explains why some predictions that we receive from our spirit friends don't seem to come true. Let me clarify this a bit more for you: If I had decided *not to accept* both of the opportunities I have told you about regarding the staff visit to Bradford and the offer of a transfer to the L.T. Publicity Department, both events would still have taken place but would not have included me. This is not because my spirit friends were wrong in forecasting what was to come for me but, because in exercising my free will choice and saying no to that which was being offered to me, I would have excluded myself from taking part in both of the events.

The two events I have outlined above came about with a gap of several years between my going on the staff trip to Bradford and later on changing my occupation to that of publicity inspector.

During those same years my family life altered in several ways and sad to say not always for the better. In the next chapter I will relate how certain changes came about in our family that would affect each and every one of us in different ways.

CHAPTER EIGHT

Up until now the main emphasis of this book has been about spiritual matters that affected our family. However, it is of the changes that took place over the years to our family that affected us all very deeply.

It is with a mixture of heartache and joy that I have to tell you of which, as I have already said, affected each of us in a different way.

We were living the life of a typical average working class family with the usual ups and downs that are the experiences of most people. For instance, I had experienced the death of my father and mother, Dee had lost her father to cancer some years ago, whilst we were still living in Luton and we had also lost various members of both our extended families.

Dee's mother lived with us for a short time after we had moved to Aveley but happily it wasn't long before she was able to qualify for a council flat in Aveley village, which was less than a mile from our house. I thought we were all set for a good future, but it was not to be.

As I told you earlier on in the book, when I met my wife, Dee, at Harrods on my return from RAF service, it was love at first sight for me so I was the lucky one. For Dee, this was not the case and although I think it fair to say she became very fond of me and probably thought in the early years of our marriage that she loved me, as time went by she found that this was not so and she felt unhappy in our marriage and wanted to find a way out of it.

This must have been very stressful for her because she was a very sensitive person and would have been torn between her own personal needs and those of her children, whom she loved dearly. She also did not want to hurt me and so she continued to live with us.

This situation continued for some years but was to change owing to the whole family suffering a traumatic loss, which I believe was the trigger for Dee making the decision to leave our family home. Here are the two events that happened which I believe caused Dee to finally put her decision to leave our family home into action:

It all began at 9pm on the evening of the 26th of June 1979 (I will never forget that time and date). I was sitting watching TV when there was a knock on the front door. I opened the door to find a policeman standing there.

He asked me if I was Mr Shave and did I have a son named Michael? I replied: "Yes" and he then suggested that he would like to step inside as he had something very important to tell me and that he would like my wife to be present.

He said he was deeply sorry to inform us that our son, Michael, had drowned early that evening in one of the local clay pits. He went on to say that he required one of us to accompany him to Orsett Hospital in order to identify the body. Fortunately, I was able to accede to his request on my own because our daughter, Deena, returned home from an evening out with her fiancé whilst the policeman was still with us.

I was, therefore, able to leave her to comfort her mother and two brothers whilst I was absent with the policeman attending to the necessary procedures at both the hospital and then the police station.

It is difficult for me to put into words the immediate shock and emotional upset that we as a family experienced on that fateful June evening. I will try, however, to give you some idea of the factors that were bound to affect each member of the family in a different way as a result of the relationship each one had with Michael. Let me explain this further:

Not only was there a shared sense of loss that we all felt as a family, there was also the very personal emotion that was experienced by each individual member of the family. This was determined by the position occupied within the family structure. When you think about it, whether you are a parent, an older brother, or younger brother or a sister, there will inevitably be differences to the emotional sense of loss that is felt by each member of the family. Age and gender also play a part as to how a person copes with bereavement and so it was with our family.

My daughter, Deena, was aged twenty at the time of Michael's passing and Glen, his older brother, was seventeen and David, his younger brother was only thirteen years of age.

Because each person's grief is so personal to them, we cannot feel exactly as they do but can only offer our love in order to try and help each of them cope with their own personal feelings.

It has often been said that no parent wishes to outlive their children and both Dee and I were, at that moment in time, experiencing how true that saying is.

It is almost impossible to find the words to describe the devastating shock we all experienced on that day and for many weeks to come because, as I have already said, all of us were faced with an emotional crisis that was slightly different and personal to each of us depending on our place in the family unit.

There is another saying that is often expressed at a time of bereavement and that is "that time will heal". It is a saying that has a certain amount of truth but, of course, in the immediate period following bereavement, it is of little use because of the painful feeling of loss and physical separation that is being experienced. This pain is also felt by Spiritualists and is not any easier to cope with by having the knowledge that life continues after death. The lack of the physical presence of a loved one who has just died is a powerful emotion for anyone to have to face and whether they are religious or otherwise, it still takes time to come to terms with their loss.

As a family, we were all now faced with a future that would not include our beloved Michael's physical presence in our family home.

Looking back at the immediate weeks that followed. I am sure that my daughter, Deena, made a decision that was definitely influenced by the recent tragedy of losing her brother, who was only fifteen years old.

She was engaged to a local young man named Derek and had been with him for about eighteen months. She quite suddenly decided to break off the engagement with him. She followed this with an equally sudden decision to return to her previous young man, Kevin Bradon. He, on hearing about Michael's death, had contacted her to offer his condolences. He had known our family for some years and had seen a great deal of young Michael and had come to know him well.

Within about five months they were married at Grays Spiritualist Centre on the 24th of November 1979. They were fortunate in being able to move into a private flat in Stifford Clays, which is about four miles from Aveley.

My wife and I were now faced with a new family situation as we now had to adjust to life without Deena and Michael's presence in our home and it proved to be too much for Dee to cope with.

As I have already told you, she had wanted to leave the marital home for quite some time and within less than five months of Deena's wedding she carried out her desire to do so. It seems strange to tell but she unwittingly chose the 1st of March 1980 as the day to leave our home. That day was our 22nd wedding anniversary.

She said she was, for the present, leaving the two boys to continue living with me and was moving to live with her mother in her one bedroom flat in Aveley village. She said that although she no longer wished to be my wife, she would continue to regard me as her best friend and hoped I would be able to accept her as such. I replied by saying I would and added that I still loved her and would be glad to have her back if she ever thought she had made a mistake in leaving me and wished to return.

Her decision to leave deeply affected both of our remaining sons, of course, but there was one thing that helped them to some extent and that was that their nan's flat was only a short distance away from us. This meant that it was easy for them to visit their mother in her new home. This could not entirely compensate them for the fact that their mother, as well as Michael and Deena, would in future no longer be sharing our family home. It is hard to image how David felt at the quick succession of events that he was faced with because he was only thirteen and five months at the time of Michael's death and soon after his fourteenth birthday he was faced with his sister leaving home to live with her husband, Kevin and now he had to face his mum's departure from the marital home.

Glen, though being a bit older than his brother David, had to deal with the same set of circumstances and although he has always been one to keep his feelings very much to himself, I believe he suffered just as much as his brother and sister did at that dreadful time in our family life.

Speaking with regards to how the series of events affected me, it was bound to be different, but no less traumatic. However, there was one thing that helped me cope with the immediate days after Michael's death and it was this: You will recall that I had been successful in being accepted for one of the vacant positions in London Transport's publicity department. It just so happened that I was required to start my new duties just five days after the day of Michael's passing.

As a result, I was so busy learning a whole new way of managing my daily life that it had the effect of helping me, to a certain degree, to manage my grief in the new circumstances in which I found myself. I think I was very fortunate because it is in those first few days that the feeling of loss is at its most powerful. That is what I found to be the case but, of course I can only speak for myself as I am fully aware that everyone's emotions are not entirely the same and can vary quite considerably with each individual who is faced with bereavement. This is doubly so when the person they have lost is not only a close relative but is also a person of such a young age.

When the person suffering the loss is the mother, the emotions are even more acutely felt than are those of the other members of the family and I believe this is because of the unique relationship a mother has with her child, which begins at the moment of conception. It is then that the wonderful bonding of mother and child begins.

From that moment on, the womb of the mother is the starting place for the new baby's spirit to begin to form its Earthly body so that in time it will be able to be born into our world of matter.

Until the time for birth arrives, this wonderful new creation shares everything with its newly-found mother. Although it is an individual spiritual being, it is, for the first nine months, confined to the womb in order that its physical body can take shape and be developed. During that period the new baby is totally dependent on the mother for everything, until the wonderful moment comes when it is time to be born.

It is at the time of birth that the new baby's spirit has a separate existence from its Earthly mother for the first time. Up until that time mother and baby were sharing their lives within the same body and that close relationship can only be experienced by a mother and her baby. It is because of this very special bond that a mother has to every one of her children, that I have described above, that no other member of the family can feel the loss of a child so deeply as does a mother.

Soon after Dee had left our marital home, she filed for a divorce, which took approximately two years to be made absolute. About a year later, I was faced with coping with a new challenge because both David and Glen had left home and so I now had to face living on my own.

David had gone to live with his mother in her recently acquired council maisonette in South Ockendon village some three miles away. He and I had a very close relationship but it was just that he quite naturally missed his mum, which is understandable.

Glen left home to join the Royal Air Force. This was occasioned by the changes that came about in his personal life. He had ever since leaving school, been employed by the Bata Shoe company in East Tilbury. The firm had been there since before the war and had built a whole village of its own surrounding the actual shoe factory.

The company decided to close its British factory down and as a result Glen was made redundant. He worked for another small firm for a short period but he did not like the conditions there. The good conditions he had been used to at Bata's factory were very much in absence in the new company. It was not long before he decided to leave and in 1983 he left to make a new life for himself in the RAF.

His service life lasted for some six years, during which time he learnt a new trade as an airframe fitter. He met and married Sharon, his first wife and they lived in married quarters until his demob in about 1989.

He found work at Luton Airport as an airframe fitter and he and Sharon were fortunate to be housed by Luton Council in one of their flats. Three years after moving into their new home, they were blessed with the birth of a baby daughter, which they named Victoria.

It would be nice to be able to tell you that they lived happily ever after but I am afraid that I can't because a short time after the happy event their marriage came to an end and Sharon returned to her family in the north of England, taking baby Victoria with her.

Not only was the parting of the ways a very unpleasant affair, it was made worse for Glen because Sharon went out of her way to put as many obstacles as she could in the way to prevent him having access to his daughter. So hard did she make it for him to see her that after some years he could not cope with the pressure anymore and so he gave up trying.

Their break up was also sad for me because not only did it hurt me to see what I thought to be a good marriage end in such a way but also right up to this present day I have never been able to meet my granddaughter and it is now some twenty-one years since her birth. Fortunately for Glen, soon after his divorce from Sharon, his mother introduced him to Alison, a young lady she was working with in Grays and in due course they fell in love and were married in 1995.

Alison and Glen were able to buy a house in Luton so that he could continue working at Luton Airport. Some years later they shared the joy of having a daughter and they named her Ella. She was born on the 27th of July 2007, which I feel was some compensation to them both for having had to face the death of Glen's mother Dee only the month before.

She had been suffering with cancer of the kidneys for some time and finally lost her battle with the dreaded decease on the 24th of June. Of course, they had hoped that she would have been able to live long enough to see her new granddaughter, but unfortunately that did not happen.

Ella is now in her fourth year and is my fifth grandchild. Her half-sister, Victoria (who she has yet to meet), is now twenty-one years of age at the time of writing. My other three grandchildren were all born to Deena and Kevin during their sixteen years of marriage. Michael is the oldest at twenty-eight years of age, Laura is the next at twenty-five and then Nicole, who is twenty-two. Until recently they all shared the same surname of Bradon, which is that of their father Kevin, but Laura has since then married a man called Stan and so is now Laura Rosenburg.

Sadly for them their mother and father were divorced in 2002 but I am glad to say they are without bitterness to either their mum or dad.

My son, David, is happily married to his second wife Jackie but as yet they have not been blessed with any children from their union; they have both been married before and Jackie has a daughter named Ami, who is temporarily away at college in Preston. David's first marriage to Sharon was childless and in hindsight it is probably fortunate that it was so in view of the fact that their union did not last, but it has made him wish all the more to be blessed with a child in his present marriage.

I would be so thrilled for them both if his wish could be granted but, of course, I realise that life cannot always turn out for us the way we want it to and that we all have to work out the way to deal with life as it is and not what we ourselves wish it to be.

Having told you how Michael's passing affected my children's lives, I will, in the following chapter, tell you first how Dee and then I myself coped with living our lives after our separation.

CHAPTER NINE

For about twenty years after Dee had left me, I saw very little of her apart from special occasions such as our children's weddings and twenty-first birthdays etc. We were invited separately to these family events owing to our changed circumstances but our children knew that we had parted company without rancour and that it would not cause any problems for us to meet on these occasions.

It is inevitable, therefore, that the following account of Dee's life during that period will not be very detailed because I have had to rely mainly on what I have learnt from our children; however, the things that I relate will be as accurate and factual as I can possibly make them. I'm afraid that once again I must apologise that I am unable to give a date to most events that she experienced after our parting because, as I have already said, it is in most cases information that I acquired from my children.

After leaving our marital home, Dee lived with her mother in her one bedroom flat in Aveley village until she was able to qualify for a council maisonette in South Ockendon village. Her application to be rehoused was helped by the fact that David, having lived for two years with me, had moved in with his mum and his nan because he was missing his mum so much. This meant that Dee was able to satisfy Thurrock Council's requirements for her and David to be rehoused.

They were happy living together in their new home which, of course, was a great improvement after having had to share a small one bedroom flat with Dee's mum.

At first David continued to attend his school in Aveley by cycling there each day. As time went on, of course, he had to leave school and start his first employment. His mother was working at Grays Police Station at that time, doing typing and general office duties.

As time went by their lives changed again. This was because Dee met a man named Keith and they began a serious relationship, which led to her accepting his proposal of marriage.

David decided to return to live with me in his old home and I was more than happy to have him back with me and I am happy to say we shared several happy years together. As time went by he, of course, was changing from boyhood to manhood and I am very proud to say that as this change came about he became not only a much loved son but also a person who I came to think of as a valued friend.

It was almost inevitable that, as time went by, he would meet someone who he would want to marry. This indeed is just what happened when he met Sharon, who was to become his first wife.

It was not long before they both set up home together in a place of their own in Grays. This, of course, meant that I was now once again the sole occupant of our family home.

During those same years, Dee had married Keith and lived with him in his bungalow in Grays but, sad to say, their marriage did not last for very long. I think from what I have been told that their personalities were so different. Dee was very spiritual in her outlook on life whereas Keith was much more materialistic and in addition to that, he proved to be very insensitive towards Dee on various occasions. This eventually led to their divorce because they were too incompatible for the marriage to continue.

On completion of the divorce, Dee was able to afford to acquire a small house in Aveley village, where she lived alone for a short time. She had kept up with her Spiritualism and had continued to sit in her development circle and had made many new friends over the years.

In addition to this, Dee had always enjoyed Country and Western music and this led her to join a line dancing club where she increased her number of friends still further.

One of the new people she met during those years was a man by the name of George. They became very close and she lived with him for a short period before, in due course, they were married.

Their first home was near to the town of Romford in Essex. They then moved to Aveley and it was there that her health started to deteriorate. She was diagnosed as having cancer of the kidneys but was not told at that stage whether or not it was terminal.

On learning of her condition, our children suggested that she contact me to help her by giving her a course of spiritual healing. She was reluctant to do so because she was unsure how her husband, George, would feel about it and also whether I would be comfortable with the idea. However, after they had all discussed it together, they decided to ask me and in fact it was George, to his credit, who made the phone call to ask me if I would consider helping Dee in her hour of need.

Of course I agreed immediately and went that very same evening to see them. She knew, of course, that I could not promise to cure her of her condition because, remember, she was a very experienced Spiritualist by this time and was well aware as to how spiritual healing works and that I would be unable to make any promises regarding the outcome of the healing.

I continued to treat her for many weeks and of course she was also receiving orthodox medical treatment for her condition. I must emphasis here that Dee was not at this stage confined to bed; in fact, she was still, in spite of her relatively poor health, able to continue living her normal daily life for quite some time.

They decided to move home and went to live first in Benfleet and then after some time moved yet again, this time to Canvey Island.

Her husband, George, though not sharing her spiritual beliefs, was quite agreeable to let her live her life as she thought fit regarding her spiritual activities. Dee was able to carry on attending her Spiritualist church and sitting in circle and going to any other functions that were of interest to her. She was able to help quite a few people with private sittings and she was also used by Spirit to relay messages to other members of her development circle, but she was unable to develop her gift of mediumship sufficiently to her own satisfaction for her to be able to serve on the platform at church services. I think this was more a case of a lack of self-confidence rather than any lack of ability; in fact, on a couple of occasions she did share the platform with an experienced medium and apparently performed very well. This gave her great satisfaction and I think renewed her ambition to eventually do some platform work. However, this was not to be because, sad to say, her health let her down.

Dee had not enjoyed good health for some years and had had several spells of having to go into various hospitals for invasive surgery. This latest health challenge, which had started back in Aveley, proved to be the re-occurrence of cancer of the kidneys which, after lots of treatment in several different hospitals over a period of some seven years, finally proved too much for her.

She passed away in Southend hospital on the 24th of June 2007 in the early hours of the morning. She had put up such a fight, which we all witnessed over her final weeks.

Some time later, my daughter, Deena, had a private sitting with a medium whose work we knew to be of a good standard and her mother was able to come through to her and so was my father.

In both cases what they had to say was very accurately communicated to her by the medium. Her mother said that, although she was aware that it was time for her to pass on; she did not really want to leave us all but was too exhausted to be able to delay her departure any longer. She, of course, sent her love to us all. Other personal things concerning Deena's life were also communicated. Then my father sent the following message, which he wished Deena to pass on to me. He said that he felt I may not have realised how much he loved me and that he had passed so quickly into the Spirit Realm that he was unable to say goodbye as he would have liked to have done. This part of the message was so accurate that I am going to devote the next part of this chapter to relate to you just how his sudden passing had happened many years earlier.

You will be able to see that there was no way the medium being used to communicate his message to Deena could have had any prior knowledge of the circumstances which took place on the day of my dad's passing. It is a good example of the evidence that is available to us all here on Earth that demonstrates without any doubt that we do indeed survive physical death because my father died on the 5th of January 1963 and Deena was receiving his message in the year 2010, some forty-six years later.

On the fateful day of his passing, I arrived at my dad and mum's flat to find him watching the Arthur Haynes Show on television. He always enjoyed a good laugh and it was good to see him perking up after a recent, very nasty chest infection that he had been suffering with over the recent Christmas holiday.

I had been in the flat only a few minutes when my mother asked me if I would like a sherry. I said: "Yes please" and so she poured out a glass for each of us. Before I took my first sip, I said: "I wish you both a Happy New Year and many more of them." Before my dad could take his first sip of the sherry, he said: "Oh! Just a minute" and managed to place his glass down on the small table next to him as he slumped forward in his chair unconscious. He was unable to watch the second half of the Arthur Haynes Show because he had passed on to the next world. His death was as sudden as that.

I hope you can see from this the accuracy of the message he was able to pass on to me via my daughter, Deena, at her sitting with the medium all those years later.

At the time of his passing, my wife and I were living in Tooting with our first two children and had not yet been introduced to Spiritualism. This meant that I, like the rest of the family, thought that my father was now dead and that there was no likelihood of seeing him again. Of course, the message received from him all those years later proved to my satisfaction that not only was he not dead but that he was now living happily in a new dimension in the Spirit World.

I learnt a very salutary lesson on the day of my dad's passing and it was thanks to my wife that I did and I have been grateful to her ever since. What I am about to tell you is a good example of the old adage that *one should never put off until tomorrow what one can do today*.

Here is what happened: Earlier on the same day that my dad died I finished my day's work at Merton Bus Garage at about one o'clock and intended to have a quick snack and then go to visit my parents. Dee knew of my intention and was not expecting me to come home until about mid-evening because we had agreed that it would be nice for me to go and see my parents straight from work. This decision was in response to a phone call we had had from my mother earlier in the week. She had said that my dad had been quite unwell over the Christmas period with a chest infection and had said that he had not seen me for some weeks.

Whilst I was having my snack in the canteen, one of the drivers asked me to have a game of snooker with him. I said: "Yes," then, I'm ashamed to admit, one game led to another and then another and by the time we had finished it was about five o'clock and as result, instead of going to my parent's house, I went home.

On arrival there, Dee said to me: "Why are you home so early" and also asked: "How is your dad?" When I told her that I had not been to see him as I had said I would and gave her my reason for not going, she quite rightly said in no uncertain terms that I should go now and not leave it until tomorrow. I'm afraid I overreacted and said: "Oh well, if you're going to nag me about it, I will" and so saying, I went out the front door shutting it firmly behind me.

What a way to learn a lesson eh? If Dee had not said that I should go in such a forthright way, I would not have been present to witness my dad's passing and even more importantly I would not have been there to help my mother in her time of need.

It is yet another item to be added to the list of the many things that I have to thank Dee for. During all those years that she shared her life with me, I have come to realise just how much she gave me and how fortunate I am to have had her in my life. For a start, she presented me with our four wonderful children, whom we were able to share many wonderful moments with as a loving family. That, of course, takes first place on the list.

A very close second on that list of gratitude is that it was because of Dee's search to find a religion that she could thoroughly believe in that I also had found and accepted Spiritualism as my religious faith.

This was to prove so very important and comforting to us both when we had to face the loss of our son, Michael, in such a tragic and shocking way. I like to think it has also helped my daughter, Deena, along with David and Glen to cope with the tragic loss of their brother.

Having given a reasonable account of Dee's life after our parting of the ways from that year in 1980 up until her sad death in 2007, I turn now to how my own life changed in that same year that we parted up until the present time. The first thing I wish to make clear is that our separation was an event that Dee wanted to happen.

The reasons for her decision to make such a dramatic change to her life are matters that I have already dealt with earlier in the book. As for myself, I was faced with having to accept the fact that to continue living together in disharmony was out of the question. It was for this reason that I reluctantly agreed to her need for us to go our separate ways.

You will recall that I had offered her the chance to return to me if in the course of time she was to regret having taken her leave of me. I realised that the taking up of my offer to return was highly unlikely because she had made it pretty clear for some time of her intention to end our relationship. I took solace from the fact that at least we had parted without bitterness between us and that neither of us blamed the other for what was about to take place in our broken relationship.

As a result of our mutual understanding that doing nothing was not an option, we agreed that the divorce application should be made on the grounds of the irretrievable breakdown of the marriage. This avoided the unpleasant subject of apportioning who was legally to blame for our marriage having become unable to continue any further.

I have already dealt with the changes that affected my children's lives in the years following Michael's passing so I will from here on concentrate mainly on myself and how my life changed as a result of the new circumstances which I now had to face as a result of our parting.

In the period immediately following Dee's departure. I was so busy keeping house for my two sons and myself and going out to work each day that I had very little time to dwell on any sorrow that I was feeling. However, I was experiencing, deep within me, considerable sadness at having been subjected to two major tragedies in my life in quick succession.

For the first couple of years I continued to attend the monthly meeting of the Romford branch of The Institute of Spiritualist Mediums. I was a life member of the ISM and both Dee and I held the ISM in high regard because it is an organisation dedicated to the promotion, teaching and development of spirit communication and had at the time been in existence for over forty years.

Up until our separation in 1980, Dee and I attended regularly every month but, of course, this was no longer the case. I am sorry to say that without her at my side my attendances were less enjoyable and I found that my enthusiasm was somewhat less than it had been up until that time. I was still, however, considered by my fellow members to be worthy of the post of becoming the chairperson for the Romford branch and over the years I accepted the post on two occasions. I was also on the head office executive committee for a year or so and took both positions very seriously and I did not miss any meetings during my terms of office.

During both the times I was in office, I had the pleasure of chairing three of the large publicity meetings that took place in the Windmill Hall, Upminster. The meetings were in addition to the normal branch meetings and were held with the purpose of promoting not only the ISM but also, of course, Spiritualism in general.

We always tried to obtain the services of well known mediums at those special meetings and I'm proud that on one of these occasions to have officiated as chairperson to the late, world famous medium, Doris Stokes.

The Windmill Hall, Upminster has a seating capacity for over three hundred people. Needless to say, every one of the seats was occupied and Doris, in spite of coming from her sick bed, still showed up for her appointment with us, so as not to let us down, She performed in her usual homely way and gave many good evidential messages. This made the evening a great success for everyone concerned.

During those same years I was still engaged with my spiritual healing work, which consisted of, in most cases, me visiting the homes of people in need of my services. This was done mainly in the evenings or sometimes at weekends because, of course, I was still in full-time employment with London Transport.

Most of my patients came to me as a result of recommendations, by word of mouth, from people who were satisfied that they had benefited from having received spiritual healing. I did not charge for my work because, being employed, I did not need to do so. Neither did I have a healing sanctuary of my own. This was partly because my time was fully occupied with attending to my family's needs in addition to my employment with LT, but also because I have always been more comfortable with attending to people's requirements in their own homes. It is the case that some people are either unable to attend a healing sanctuary because of their disability or are just people who prefer the privacy of their own home.

In 1980, I applied to become a full member of The Essex Healers Association. I was in due course accepted for membership because of references that I was able to present to them. Among the references was one from Don Hatch, who was still holding office as the president of the Grays Spiritualist Centre and because he by that time had known me for twelve years. He was able not only to vouch for my good character, but was also aware of my healing work and so was well qualified to speak on my behalf.

I mentioned early on in the book on page twenty-six, that it was Don Hatch who was in the chair at the very first Spiritualist meeting that I attended along with my neighbours, Bill and Iris Green and their young lodger, Sharon. It was as a direct result of what took place at that meeting that both Dee and myself were motivated to seek further knowledge of Spiritualism.

In addition to the reference from Don Hatch, there was a very important letter of recommendation that I was able to enclose with my application for membership of the Essex Healing Association. It came from a very grateful man by the name of Ron Ilines, who had received and benefited from spiritual healing with my help on two occasions. The second time proved to be life-saving for him.

I shall tell you of what took place with regards to the healing he received in great detail in the next chapter, not only because it is a significant part of my experience as a healer, but more importantly the result of the healing Ron received is a splendid example of what can be achieved when spiritual healing is applied in favourable conditions.

In the first part of the chapter, I will attempt to show where all kinds of non-orthodox healing sits within the scope of healing in general at this moment in time. I also want to show how it took many long years of struggle for acceptance before it arrived at its modern day status.

I suppose this should not surprise anyone who has any knowledge of the history of medicine. We know that it took a great struggle to get just the basics of hygiene and cleanliness to be accepted in our hospitals by the establishment of the day. Surgeons and other members of the medical fraternity were very slow to see the merits of the case that was being made by the more enlightened members of their own fraternity.

The consequences of this lack of hygiene were that many people, on arriving at hospital, became more ill within a short space of time than when they had first been admitted. Many of them, sadly, went on to die.

As time went by these new ideas found favour and were adopted and as a result medical practice has become more and more able to adapt to new medical practices. The results are apparent for all to see.

I have already mentioned that each human being is a spirit with a body that is matter. It is the spiritual part of us that controls how our body functions and because we have God given free will, it is sometimes inevitable that we don't always make the choices that are either in our own, or indeed other people's, best interests.

This explains to some extent why in the case of medical progress, as I have outlined above, it has been hindered in its progression. It was as a result, in many a case, simply of the wrong choice having been made.

There is a very true long established saying that says *we should learn from our mistakes*. We have been told over many years by our guides in Spirit that it is when we are suffering great adversity that it is then that we learn the most. It is part of the great natural law that governs everything in our universe.

CHAPTER TEN

It is very clear that there are many aspects to healing and that the main form of healing that most people think of when that word is mentioned is the type of healing that they receive when they visit their family doctor or attend their local hospital etc. It is absolutely understandable that this is so because it is fortunately the case that the majority of people are able to receive everything they need with regards to their medical care by simply visiting their local GP or hospital. This means that most people do not need to have to consider using alternative methods of treatment.

Modern medicine is constantly adapting its methods in response to the ever-changing conditions with which it is faced in the modern world. This evolution of medical practices means that the medical profession can offer treatments that are forever improving their ability to be able to help their patients and this improvement is as a direct result of the increased knowledge that has been gained by it over many years. We are all, at this moment in time, fortunate to be able to be treated and cured of ailments that a few years ago would have been considered as life-threatening.

This is, of course, all very good and wonderful and no doubt this natural progression will continue because medicine, just like everything else in the universe, is controlled by the natural law of evolution. However, there are many factors that must be considered when faced with the need to maintain good health. First and foremost is that we should all accept *personal responsibility for the way we live our daily lives*. This can be summed up in as little as one word - LIFESTYLE. Without going into a long list of dos and don'ts, we can all think of the many things that we should or should not do to maintain good health.

The medical profession, even with all the skills and knowledge it has at its disposal, cannot help us if we choose not to accept the advice and the treatments that we are being offered. There are other factors beyond the physical which also have to be considered. There is the mental and psychological state of the patients to be taken into account and it is a fact that, over the years, this side of medical practice has played an increasing role in the treatment of illness. But the present relationship between the two approaches in deciding the appropriate treatment that is required when treating patients was not arrived at easily. It had to be fought for with great determination over many years by those doctors within the medical profession who wished to use the psychological approach to patients illnesses in addition to that of just their physical requirements.

It is natural and quite reasonable for the medical fraternity to have a cautious approach to new methods but to be hostile to new ideas and methods of treatment without good reason is plainly unacceptable. They were in a dilemma between caution on the one hand and a resistance to new ideas on the other. It took many years to be resolved and sadly, as a result, many new treatments took a great length of time to be accepted and introduced. Happily, it is the case that, with the increase over the years of scientific knowledge to help them, the medical profession can nowadays make a more informed assessment of new treatments that are presented to them.

This means, of course, that these days it is quite the normal practice for patients to be referred by their doctor to those specialists who work in the field of psychiatric conditions in addition to those of their colleagues, who are concerned in dealing mainly with the physiological side of the patients needs.

There are still, however, even to the present day, some branches of medical practices that are not as yet fully accepted by the medical authorities. For instance, homeopathy and acupuncture have only partial recognition by the governing bodies and this reluctance towards new techniques can vary from country to country.

This reluctant approach by the medical authorities becomes especially apparent when it comes to what is usually referred to as 'alternative medicine'.

The word *alternative* is, however, somewhat misleading because it should always be the case that patients receiving treatments that are other than that of orthodox medical practice are in fact receiving *complimentary* treatment and that should mean that both disciplines are working in close cooperation with one another.

I wish to make it abundantly clear that none of the recognised spiritual healing associations would instruct or agree to any of their members giving healing to a person as an *alternative* to normal medical practice. This also means that healers should never suggest to patients that they discontinue taking any medicines that have been prescribed by their doctor.

I would also like to clear up another widely held misconception - that *spiritual healing* is the same as *faith healing*, because this is not so.

People are not required to have faith to receive spiritual healing, neither are they required to have any particular religious affiliation. The absence of religious belief by the person receiving the healing has no bearing whatsoever as to the success or otherwise of the treatment being applied. The person who is receiving the healing could, for instance, be in a coma or receiving the treatment from a healer some distance away because a request for them to receive it was made by a loved one without the patient's knowledge. It could also be the case that it is a baby who is receiving the healing, or even a dog, or cat, or indeed any other animal. Spiritual healing isn't restricted to human beings only. This shows quite clearly that faith by the person receiving the healing is not required for healing to take place. However, this does not mean that faith plays *no* part in the healing process, far from it. The part that faith plays in the healing of the sick by spiritual healing is to be found in the recognition by the healer that they can be used by God via his helping angels in the world of Spirit to channel the healing rays to those in need. This process of channelling the healing was put into a wonderful quotation, which said it is a case of "FROM SPIRIT, VIA SPIRIT, TO SPIRIT".

God's love for all of his creatures, including Mankind, is unconditional and is available to everyone, whatever their beliefs are. I know this to be true because I have had personal experience of the methods which I have outlined above.

Over the years, I have been involved with the application of healing in a variety of ways. I have been used on many occasions to heal on a one-to-one basis by direct contact with patients, as well as from a distance. I have also been involved with helping to heal animals.

The gift of healing is a form of mediumship and it is used to pass on healing rays in a similar method to that which is used by mediums when being used to communicate messages from people in the realms of Spirit to their loved ones here on Earth.

There are many types of mediumship being used by a wide variety of people. It follows, therefore, that all these people, although they are engaging in the same activity, will have their own individual abilities and approaches with regards to how they are able work with God and his spirit helpers who live on the Spirit plane.

This is quite understandable because no two people are alike in any other field of activity or profession, so it is to be expected that mediums have differing abilities when it comes to the gift of spirit healing or any of the forms of communication or spiritual work.

Before I go on to relate my own experiences as a healer, I want to make a further important thing clear and it is with regards to the expected effectiveness of the treatment about to be offered and administered by any healer.

No healer should ever promise a cure for whatever the patient's malady happens to be because the amount of benefit any patient is able to receive from spiritual healing is determined by many factors that are beyond the scope of the healer to have any influence over.

The only promise I give to my patients is that I will continue to attend to their needs for as long as they wish me to. I consider the part played by the healer in the process of healing can be likened to the links in a chain. The removal of just one of the links of a chain will render it unable to carry out the function it was designed for, which is to transmit a source of power from one part of a mechanism to another. In the case of spiritual healing, the healer can be viewed as the person who is the final link in the chain. The power of all healing comes from the same source, as does everything else that exists in the cosmos. It comes from God.

Healing is a wonderful example of his natural law at work. God helps us to overcome our illnesses in a variety of ways, as I have already to some extent explained. Whether it is by using those people who are doctors and nurses, who are involved in what is known as orthodox medicine, to heal the sick or by directing

His love and healing through other people who are dedicated to using spiritual healing, or indeed any of the other methods of healing. The method is basically the same whoever the person or persons are that are involved in the process of healing.

The healing is transmitted from God via His spiritual helpers in the world of Spirit and finally, through the doctors or healers, to the person in need of the healing.

I have already told you how I was introduced to healing and also how I was encouraged to become personally involved with its application. I think it was in about 1969 that I began my healing work and I gradually learned over the next few years that I was able to help people by asking God to include me in the process of healing the person who was in need of it.

The results of my healing work varied as to the amount of success I was able to achieve, as it does with anyone engaged in the process of healing because, as I hope I have already made clear, it is not within our power to decide the outcome of our administrations as healers. This is because we people on the Earth plane cannot see the whole picture when it comes to helping others. This is especially so in the healing process because everyone who receives healing is a unique individual and receives healing that is suited to their particular personal need. This goes some way to explaining why some people who seem to have what appears to be an identical illness as another person has often cannot be helped in quite the same way.

Over my years as a healer, I was able to help all kinds of people to some degree. This was sometimes very apparent and was achieved in a very short space of time. In other cases the amount of healing received was not so obvious and took longer to achieve. There was, however, inevitably a small number of cases where the healing seemed not to have been successful.

The healing that I am about to tell you of is the one I am most pleased to have been associated with and because of the wonderful result of the treatment he received. I am going to tell you about it in great detail because I think it deserves to be presented in just such a way. It is a wonderful example of just what spiritual healing can achieve.

Many of the people I was able to help in the earlier years of my healing were people who were working at Hornchurch Bus Garage at the same time as myself. Among the people I helped was a driver named Ron Ilines. He was suffering at the time with a small hiatus hernia and after a short course of treatment he was cured. He introduced me to one of his neighbours, a lady called Doris Smith, whom he had told about his successful healing experience. As a result of being introduced to her, I was soon visiting her home each week to give healing to her and other people who were her friends and neighbours. These visits went on for some years and during that time Ron had given up driving buses and was given different employment which, though still with London Transport, involved him having to move out of Hornchurch Bus Garage to work elsewhere. As a result of this move, I lost touch with him.

You will remember that in the year 1979, within days of losing my son Michael, I transferred my employment from Hornchurch Bus Garage to the LT Publicity Department and from then on I was based in one of the offices at Walthamstow Bus Garage and was now working regular hours which, of course, helped me to give a better commitment to my healing work.

It was in the latter part of that same year that I received a phone call from Doris. She said that Ivy (Ron Ilines' wife) had just phoned her to ask her to ask me if I would be prepared to come and give Ron healing as he was now out of hospital and back home. I said: "Yes of course" and asked her if she knew what was wrong with him. She replied in a somewhat surprised tone of voice: "Haven't you heard?" and then went on to tell me that Ron had recently been in hospital to have an operation to remove his bladder and that he had now been sent home. The surgeon had informed Ivy that the cancer that they had found on opening him up was too far advanced for further treatment and that there was nothing more that they could do for him. Ivy was told that his life expectancy was about six months and that anything more than that must be considered as a bonus.

I, of course, was more than a little shocked on hearing this news and said as much to Doris. She asked: "Didn't you know Ron was in hospital?" I replied: "No" and explained to her that I had lost touch with him ever since he had transferred out of Hornchurch Bus Garage. She then told me that although his family knew that the cancer had been diagnosed as terminal, Ron did not know of this but of course, he was aware that he had cancer.

He said to Ivy: "You remember how Paul was able to help me a couple of years ago when I had that hiatus hernia? Well perhaps he can help again."

He asked Ivy to get in touch with me to ask if I would be willing to call on him to help him with his present condition.

Ivy was able to go along to Doris's bungalow, which is only three doors away from her own bungalow, to ask her in person to get in touch with me on her behalf because she did not want Ron to overhear what was being said if she used her own phone, especially as his condition had been diagnosed as terminal.

Within a day or so I was able to make my first visit to Ron's home in response to Ivy's request for healing. The fact that I had been informed that Ron was unaware of his cancer being diagnosed as terminal meant that I was able to speak more easily with him. He was in bed when I arrived but I was pleased to hear that he was not restricted to it and so was fully able to get out to answer nature's call etc. Though still weak from his recent treatment in hospital, he was also getting out to sit in his back garden for a short period each day.

The first thing I needed to know was how he was feeling and whether he was in any pain. He said he was not in any pain but said that he was in some discomfort owing to the fact that the incision that had been made for the removal of his bladder had not yet fully healed up and as a result of this a male nurse was visiting him each day to examine his wound and to change the dressing on it. Further to this, he had been fitted with a urinal bag, which he would have to use for the rest of his life. He quite understandably had not yet been able to fully come to terms with this new necessity in his life. It was not only a great shock for him but also he realised that it was possible that in future it may at times prove to be a frustration and an inconvenience to him.

Having satisfied myself as to his condition, I was now ready to apply the first session of healing and in view of both the condition of his wound and his having to use a urinal bag, I decided it was not convenient or practical to expect Ron to leave his bed to sit in a chair, or even for him to sit up in bed. I, therefore, told him to remain laying on his back in bed and I just held his hand instead of the laying on of hands, which is the normal method that most healers use.

It was very helpful that Ron remembered what had taken place when I had given him healing for his hiatus hernia condition some years earlier. He knew that all he was required to do was to relax whilst the healing was being given.

I was now able to apply myself to the job in hand which, of course, was to ask God to send healing to Ron for his cancer condition. I usually give a brief description of what the condition of the patient is and then I relax as much as I can in the knowledge that my helpers in the world of Spirit will be directed to assist in the healing process.

I always offer a prayer for help silently, not only because it is not necessary to speak it out loud, but also because it helps the person who is receiving the healing to relax. Healing is always greatly helped if peaceful conditions can be provided whilst it is being administered.

The method I used, as described above, is the method I would be using in the coming weeks for my visits to Ron. It is the same method I use whenever I am being used for healing. I have found over the years that it has proven to be very successful for me in working the way I have outlined and that it has also proven to be acceptable to my spirit helpers with whom I work and also to the people I have given healing to over the years. In most cases (unlike Ron), the people receiving treatment are usually able to sit on a stool or chair, but that is the only difference. I have found, over time, that the average length of time I am used for healing each patient is about twenty minutes or so.

On my second or third visit to Ron, he told me that he had something special to tell me concerning his wound that up to now had showed no sign of healing up. I am not sure whether what I am about to relate to you happened earlier the same day as my visit or whether it was a day or so earlier. It is not of importance when it happened so much as what took place when it did happen. Here is what Ron told me in his own words (as far as I can remember them now, some thirty-two years later).

I quote him as follows: "I was lying in bed attempting to read the morning paper after having enjoyed a light breakfast, which had been proceeded by a sound night's sleep when I found that I had difficulty in keeping my eyes open to carry on reading. I must have dozed off because some time later the next thing I was aware of on waking was an odour which seemed very close to me. I looked down at my stomach area and gently lifted the surgical dressing on my wound and I saw what I can only describe as a little chipolata-shaped discharge from the wound." He then said: "Without thinking, I carefully pulled at it. Fortunately, it did not hurt me and so I just laid it on the dressing. I noticed that my regular visit by the male nurse who cleans and dresses my wound was due in just a few minutes so I was able to leave it where it was for him to see. He has a key to the front door, which enables him to let himself in, because Ivy is usually out at work when he calls."

He went on to tell me that when the nurse arrived and saw what was by now the disintegrating discharge, he declared that in all his years as a nurse he had not seen anything quite like it and said that he would like Ron's doctor to see it.

A home visit was arranged and speedily carried out by the doctor. He made no comment about the nature of the discharge but said he was happy for the visits by the nurse to continue as previously arranged.

From that moment on things began to change for the better and the wound went on to heal up completely. This was followed by Ron beginning to feel stronger each day that passed. He was able to stay out in his garden for longer periods. In addition to this, he had been attending a consultant in one of the London centres for cancer. He was taken there by a hospital car service and had previously found it to be a very tiring experience. When he next went, he found that he was able to cope with the journey without so much fatigue. I, for my part, was continuing to call on Ron each week and was very pleased to see the marked change for the better that was by now very apparent.

He soon became due for his follow-up visit to the hospital where he had had his operation to remove his bladder. It was the same hospital that had sent him home with a life expectancy of approximately six months because they felt that they could do nothing more for him.

Ron attended the appointment as arranged and what a wonderful surprise it turned out to be for everyone concerned! After carrying out all the tests that were necessary to observe the progress of the cancer cells that they had had to leave in his body after the removal of his bladder, they could not find any. There was no trace of any cancer to be found and it was, therefore, decided by the doctors that no further medical treatment was required other than periodical check-ups.

Ron attended hospital regularly over the following fourteen years in order that his condition could be kept under review. He went on to live for some thirty years after the date of his original operation. He finally died on the 10th of February 2009 at the age of 81.

I have recently had the pleasure of visiting Ron's wife, Ivy, who is still living in that same bungalow in Hornchurch where Ron received the wonderful healing for his cancer. She was able to verify the things I have told you about and was able to add the details concerning his aftercare treatment and the date of his passing. Ivy is now herself eighty-one years old. She told me that for a number of years after his cancer ordeal Ron was able to continue with light duties at work.

Before I move on to other aspects of my life, I want to tell you about one more healing experience that I was personally involved with, which is again a wonderful example of just how effective spiritual healing can be.

The healing took place only three doors away from that of Ron Ilines and it concerned Ernie Smith (he was the husband of Doris, mentioned above). I was able to help him as follows: He had been for some time having difficulty in controlling his bladder movements and was taking tablets prescribed by his doctor to control his condition. In spite of this, his discomfort was continuing to get worse and he informed his doctor of this. He also mentioned to him that he and his wife were looking forward in the very near future to going on a three month holiday to visit relatives in the USA and that he was concerned that he might become worse and require hospital treatment whilst they were there. The doctor said: "Don't forgo your holiday, I will give you extra medication to take with you and then, on your return, I will see about a hospital appointment if it proves to be necessary."

Ernie and Doris went off to America as planned but, unfortunately, after only three weeks they were obliged to return home. This was because Ernie's bladder condition had by then not only become a good deal worse but was also now causing him considerable pain. As a result of this, he was now experiencing an interrupted sleep pattern and when he needed to urinate he found it difficult to do so.

Having been told about his condition, I went to see him to see if he would like me to give him some healing. On my arrival at his home, Doris let me in and led me to the lounge where Ernie was. He was slumped in an armchair and was obviously in quite some pain. He said he would be pleased if I would try to see if I could help him by giving him some spiritual healing in an attempt to ease his pain.

He also told me that in a few days' time he was due to attend hospital so that his condition could be diagnosed for a possible prostate gland operation to be carried out.

I then commenced to give him spiritual healing by the laying on of my hands, as is my usual practice. I was very soon aware that my breathing slowed to a regular rhythm, as it usually does when I ask God for healing to be sent to whoever I am with. I was also aware that my hands felt very warm. Again, this is what I often experience when I am engaged in healing people. After about twenty minutes or so, I felt that I had done all that was required for the present. I then asked Ernie, in his own time, to open his eyes so that he could return to his normal consciousness. On doing so, he remarked that my hands had seemed to be giving off a great heat. I said that I was aware of this and went on to explain to him that the people who are receiving spiritual healing often feel such a sensation.

A day or two had passed when Doris phoned me to tell me the following: She said: "After you left the other evening, Ernie went to bed and not only did he have an uninterrupted nights sleep until he woke up at 9am, but in addition to that, on going to the lavatory, he was able to urinate as normal. He found that he was not in any pain and this is still the case."

When Ernie went for his hospital appointment the following week, the doctors could find nothing wrong with him. He was discharged and was not required to attend hospital for any further treatment and went on to enjoy the rest of his retirement without further trouble.

Ernie lived for quite a time after the illness I have told you about. He finally passed on as a result of a heart attack, which he suffered whilst watching the Grand National on television.

The two healing events I have just told you of were not only great examples of spiritual healing at its best but were so rewarding for me. I do not mean in a financial way, but in the spiritual sense of the word.

Over the earlier years since I became a Spiritualist, I was privileged to be able to help many people with spiritual healing. However, as the years passed, I found that my spiritual work began to change and I think, on looking back, that it was triggered by the domestic changes that had taken place, not only in my domestic situation that I have already told you about, but also because of the changes that were taking place where I worked.

The London Transport Executive, which had originally been established in the year 1933 (though was then known as the London Passenger Transport Board), was sold off to various private companies.

The new arrangements were that the bus operations within the Greater London area would in future be carried out by individually privately owned bus companies. The London Underground would in future be operated separately from these bus companies by the new Transport For London organisation, which would still, however, have the overall responsibility for all transport matters within Greater London.

These changes affected the department where I worked to a considerable degree and I found that my own duties were affected accordingly and as a result I was less happy with the way I would in future be expected to work.

The publicity department would from now on be obliged to work with several different bus companies instead of just LT central buses. This meant that several of the long-established working patterns that had been in place over many years were no longer suitable for the new set up.

In addition to this, Transport For London decided that they needed to cut down on staff requirements in various departments and so they introduced a voluntary staff severance scheme.

I decided to accept severance because my future position within the publicity department seemed to me at that moment in time to be somewhat uncertain. I left in 1987, having completed just over 25 years' service.

In the following chapter, I will try and explain to you how the above decision would be the start of my spiritual work taking a new direction.

CHAPTER ELEVEN

Having left my job, I was now fifty-one years of age and not very clear as to what I wanted to do regarding my future employment. I, of course, had the benefit of my lump sum severance pay in my bank but whilst that was some comfort to me, it was not sensible to attempt to use it to live on for any length of time. What I needed to do was to find a job to provide me with an income.

I am not going to go into much detail regarding the different jobs that I had from 1987 up until my retirement because, in general, the jobs are not relevant to the theme of this book. However, there is one way that what I did regarding my employment over those first few years was to have an affect on my spiritual activities.

I was so engrossed with paying attention to my financial needs that I am sorry to admit that in doing so I rather neglected my spiritual life. I let my membership of the Essex Healers lapse and also in those years I did not go to the ISM as much as I had done over previous years.

On reaching my retirement age this situation changed and I resumed attending the Romford branch of the ISM, and in due course became the branch chairperson and I also became a member of the National Executive Committee.

It was soon after this that I was asked to write an article for inclusion in the ISM journal, which is published quarterly. I was pleased to accept the invitation and to date I have written twenty articles. They seem to be well accepted by the readership and I also send copies of them to several mediums that I know, as well as to friends and family.

The articles are, what are known as 'inspirational writings'. When I sit down to write, I have no idea as to the words I am going to write. In most cases I mentally receive the title that my spirit friends want me use before I put pen to paper. But on occasions I have just been inspired to write the article and on reading it through after having completed it I have then been able to choose a fitting title for the article myself based on the theme and content of the article.

These articles are, at the present time, my main work for Spirit. I feel that I have been guided by events to carry out the writing of these articles by my friends in Spirit. In this way, I hope to be used to spread the knowledge of Spiritualism to help people who would perhaps not have been introduced to the subject previously. It is for this same reason that I have written this book in the format that I have, with the emphasis being mainly to give an account of the various spiritual happenings that have taken place to me and my wife and family over the years.

I am not a famous person and for that reason I cannot expect the publishers of the written word to be very interested in wanting to publish my book. They are mostly on the lookout for works written by famous people who will be in much greater demand by the reading public than those that are written by unknown authors such as myself. This is especially so in the case of religious books, which are usually classified as specialist reading, which is not considered likely to be in such demand as are biographies of well known people etc.

This means that many unknown writers cannot usually afford the money to cover the up-front costs that are required by publishers, unlike the well known writers and other famous people who are not only often not required to find these up-front charges by their publishers but often receive, in many cases, an advance payment for their book.

Because of the important part that Spiritualism has played in my life, I was determined to find a way to overcome the challenge of the cost of getting my work published that every new unknown author is faced with when they are attempting to get their book published and the fact you have been able to obtain a copy of my book to read is witness to the fact that I have succeeded to a limited degree in my endeavour by publishing it as a book.

The Spiritualist philosophy has given me peace of mind in knowing that the life we all share on this planet of ours is controlled by an ever-loving God through His *natural Law of Cause and Effect*. It has given me a better understanding of the things of matter as well as the those of Spirit and that it is Spirit that motivates all life and controls all forms of evolution that are found throughout the cosmos.

It has given me the understanding that The Great Spirit that is God is within all of creation and that although we may be unaware of it, our universe is evolving as it should. Spiritualism has also given me a better understanding of the origins of other religions and I believe that all religions are motivated by love and goodwill to Mankind. It has also helped to confirm my previously held belief that faith in the existence of God is strengthened if it is based on the wonders of his creation rather than if it is based on the written words that are found in any of the so-called holy books that are, to say the least, of doubtful origin and sadly have caused so much strife and divided loyalties throughout our world.

I am satisfied that Spiritualism offers evidence that is sound and undeniable to support its tenets of survival of life after death and that communication between the two worlds is a fact that can be proven. It is essential, however, to approach the subject of Spiritualism and its beliefs in survival after physical death with an open mind.

It is preferable to conduct your own investigations into it so that you can make an unbiased evaluation of its philosophy. I have throughout this book described how I myself went about the task of looking into it along with my wife. You will recall how our individual approach to the subject was somewhat different because my wife, Dee, was looking to find a new religion that she could be happy to embrace as her pathway through life. I, on the other hand at that time, considered myself to be a Deist, but I was happy to go along with her investigation. My motivation was based more on curiosity rather than any desire to change my religious beliefs. But in addition to considering myself to be a Deist, I have always had (right from my school days) a great interest in science and was determined that my own approach to Spiritualism would be based on using logic, together with science and reason. It was as a result of adopting this approach that I found, as time passed, that it was sensible for me to change my own religious belief because this new philosophy I was now becoming more and more familiar with satisfied my own sense of reason.

I found that all three of the requirements I have mentioned above are there in abundance within the Spiritualist philosophy and as time passed I decided that its basic tenets that life continues after physical death and that those who are now living in the Spirit Realms can indeed, when given suitable conditions, communicate with people here on the Earth plane. It is a fact that is based on sound evidence and is not just some wishful thinking by the many thousands of folk who attend Spiritualist churches.

This change in my belief did not come about quickly, but was a gradual process that was based on many experiences that both Dee and I had witnessed for ourselves during those early years. Some of these I have already told you about in the first few chapters of this book but what I want to do now is to outline for you the continuity of interest that our spirit friends show to us once we have learned how to co-operate with them to carry out our spiritual work in whatever way is appropriate to achieve a successful outcome. This may be in connection with our healing work or it could be to do with the communicating of messages either from Spirit, or to Spirit.

The following example is my own personal experience and once again I am going to tell you about it in great detail because it is a really good example of the *continuity of Spirit* that I mentioned above. It is concerned with both healing and receiving a message from Spirit:

You will remember that I told you in chapter three of how we moved from Luton and came to live next door to Bill and Iris Green in Aveley and you will, of course, also recall that it was Bill and Iris who, together with their lodger, Sharon, went with me to Grays Spiritualist Centre.

It was some time after that that Bill and Iris moved a couple of miles away and we rather lost touch with them. A few years later, Iris phoned me to ask if I could help Bill by visiting their home in order to give him some healing. She went on to inform me that he had for some time been suffering from very widespread cancer and was in some considerable pain.

Of course, I responded to her call as soon as I was able to. On arrival, I saw Bill and realised immediately just how ill he was and although I gave him healing and hoped he would get at least an easing of the pain he was suffering, I did not expect that he would survive his terrible illness for very much longer. I am sorry to say that I was right and Bill passed on a day or so later.

When Iris phoned me to say that Bill had died, she said that Bill and herself wished to thank me for responding to her call and giving him healing. She went on to tell me that she knew in her heart that it was probably too late for him to benefit very much as she was aware that she had left it too late in getting in touch with me. I replied saying that I was so sorry not to have been able to do more for him. She then said: "Oh, but you did help him, because from the moment you started the healing, he suffered no further pain." She went on to tell me that just before he passed he had called her to his bedside and said: "I am going to meet my mother now" and then, with some other words of endearment to her, he slipped peacefully away. She said that she was sure that it was the healing that he had received that enabled him to die without any further pain.

Some years later, I was on a shopping trip in Romford and I had some time to kill. This was on a Thursday and I remembered that the Romford Spiritualist Church have a midweek service each week in the afternoon on that day. Although I had not planned to attend the service, I decided to go and enjoy some time there. I arrived a few minutes before the service was due to start and I asked the lady on the door who the medium was for that afternoon. She said that it was Lee Lacy. I knew then that it would be worth staying for the service because I had seen him work at Grays Spiritualist Centre on several occasions. He always gave a good talk, which usually contained a touch of humour and his clairvoyance was of a high standard. He said that working with humour in this way seemed to help him to work with his spirit guides more easily.

When introducing Lee to the congregation, the chairperson said: "Lee will now give us a short address." On rising to his feet Lee said: "I can't resist that can I?" and followed with the words: "Number ten, Downing Street." This is typical of his humorous approach when giving his talks and his joke was well received by everyone present. During the part of the service, whilst he was giving his clairvoyance, he selected me. He said: "As I link with you, I have a man named Bill with me, can you accept him?"

I replied: "Yes." He then said: "He is totally surrounded by letters" and then asked me if I knew why would that be? I replied: "Yes," because he was a postman when he was alive. He then said: "Well Bill wants to thank you for what you did for him a short time before he passed to Spirit" and he asked me if I understood what Bill was referring to. I replied: "Yes I do" (of course, he was referring to the healing session I had had with him). He next said: "Bill is asking me to ask you when are you going to fix that letterbox?"

I knew exactly what Bill was referring to (I had recently fitted a new letterbox to my front door and it tended to remain open when the postman had put the mail through). I laughed and replied that I would attend to getting it fixed. I gave my response to Bill's question out loud to Lee and it evoked a ripple of laughter from the congregation. They were probably thinking that it was quite a clever way for him to add extra proof that it was indeed Bill the *ex-postman* who was communicating.

Bill was able to send his love to both me and my family before it was time for Lee to move on to the next person in the congregation waiting to receive a communication from friends or family in the Spirit World.

I hope that in relating the content of my message received from Bill in some detail that I have been able to illustrate clearly what I referred to as *the continuity of Spirit* that is shown to us by our friends in Spirit. In case I haven't, let me explain a little further. What I am trying make clear to you is that Bill and I first met in 1968 when Dee and I arrived in Aveley and moved in next door to him. Some years later, Bill and Iris chose to move and although they were living not far away, we more or less lost touch with them. After a few years had passed, Bill was in need of the healing and again it was some years later after his passing that, on the spur of the moment, I went into the Romford church and received the message from Bill that I have just told you about. These events took place over a period of nearly twenty years and that is what I mean by *continuity of Spirit*.

I am sure that this sequence of events did not just happen by chance. I am also sure that Iris was influenced to telephone me for help by her spiritual guide in the Spirit Realm. Likewise, I too was influenced to go into the church that day in order that I could receive Bill's message.

Let me make it clear, however, that although our friends in Spirit will do all they can to help us in any given situation, they cannot interfere with our own free will. I have already explained how this works on pages 58 to 60 of this book so I won't go into it any further now, but if you are still unclear as to what I mean, you may find it helpful to read those pages again.

I have pointed out earlier on in the book that it's quite understandable that members of our family who have already preceded us to the world of Spirit should continue to take a great interest in us and want to ensure our wellbeing where possible. But what I may not have made clear is that our guides and helpers in the world of Spirit. have this same concern for us and use their influence whenever it is possible and appropriate to prompt us to do certain things that are in our best interests.

The method they use to achieve this is *thought transference* and it is used more often than we on the Earth plane realise. A good example of this is what I have told you about in the above events that took place in Romford that day. Remember, I was in the town and had been shopping. I had not intended to go to the Spiritualist church when I suddenly remembered that it was Thursday and that the church just across the road from where I was standing held a regular service on that day. I decided there and then to go and spend some time there and I have told what happened as a result of my sudden impulse to go into the church.

I hope you can see more clearly now just how the events that I have told you of in the last few paragraphs were more than likely motivated by our friends in Spirit, who knew that Bill Green wanted to let me know that, just prior to his passing, I had helped him more than I was aware of with the healing that he had received on that day.

You can understand, I hope, how thrilled I was to receive from Bill, himself, the conformation of what his wife Iris had told me about all those years previously regarding my healing visit to him, which was that he had received help immediately after the healing was applied and that he was without further pain right up until he passed to Spirit several days later.

This thought transference I have described is something I am pretty sure you, dear reader, have experienced taking place many times in your life without you realising just what was happening. To try and explain what I mean, I want you to reflect back on the number of times throughout your life that you have heard people say: "I don't know what made me think it" and then go on to tell you of something they did or said. Another example is where a person relates something to you that they did, or had experienced and then adds the words: "I don't know what made me go there, but I just did." Often these promptings from our spirit friends are very beneficial, not only to the recipient of the thought, but also sometimes to a third person who benefits from the action you have just taken as a direct result of receiving the thought.

This last example is exactly what happened in the account I gave you above. The thought quite suddenly entered into my mind to visit Romford Spiritualist Church. I acted on that thought and as a result both Bill and myself benefited from my attendance at the service on that day.

The power of thought governs everything we humans do throughout our lives, from the many trivial things we do, to the very complicated and complex things we may be required to deal with from time to time.

Another really good example of *thought transference* is inspirational writing. I have already mentioned my own experience of this gift. I have, over the last few years, been inspired by my spirit helpers to write some twenty articles. I have told you of how I have no idea, before commencing to write, what the theme of the forthcoming article will be about.

What takes place on those occasions is that I am inspired to write the words that Spirit send to me by the process of thought transference.

All inspirational writing is achieved in this way as is the composing of music, writing novels and all of the many inventions and artworks that Mankind has benefited from over the years. I don't wish to minimise in any way the part that is played by these gifted composers, poets and inventors. Far from it, because they are all very special people who have been inspired to give the world so many wonderful things. I am merely trying to give you some idea as to how this co-operation between the people who are on the Earth plane, together with our friends in the Spirit World, have been inspired to achieve so many wonderful things over the many years of Mankind's existence.

I firmly believe that all the great things that have been achieved throughout the history of Mankind, in whatever field of endeavour you choose to consider, have been spiritually inspired and that the progress and continuing inventiveness of the human race is a direct result of this inspiration having been received and then acted upon in whatever way is found to be suitable for the benefit of everyone.

This principle applies to all the great people who have been inspired throughout the ages, whether in the field of music, science, art or the written word. I include also the much maligned politicians in this process because there have been and still are many great souls who are dedicated to the well-being of Mankind within that profession too.

Conclusion: I feel that I have by now written a sufficient amount about the shared events in the lives of both Dee and myself that persuaded both of us to become convinced believers in the truth of the Spiritualist philosophy, which demonstrates with plenty of evidence to confirm it, that life continues after physical death.

I have tried to be as accurate as I possibly can in relating all the many events that we both experienced; however, as I said earlier on in the book, I have not always been able to give a date to some particular events because of the time lapse between the actual events taking place and my relating them to you, the reader. To overcome this problem, I decided to try and relate what took place in such a detailed way that the reader would have no doubt as to what had taken place so that a sound verdict can be arrived at when considering the evidence being offered as proof.

I hope that what I have written about will enable you, the reader, to decide whether what I have told of is reasonable and is based on logical evidence that you will find acceptable. If you are unable to accept the ideas I have presented to you with honesty and sincerity, then, of course, you are free to come to your own conclusions, but I suggest that any decision to reject the Spiritualist philosophy would need some rational alternative hypothesis to be considered as a valid critique of Spiritualist values.

All religions include many ideas that they all share in common, irrespective of what the denomination happens to be. The two most commonly shared ideas are that first, there is a God that is responsible for all of creation and secondly, that life continues after death.

Where the Spiritualist religion differs to the mainstream religions is not in the two ideas mentioned above but that it is able to prove by introducing evidence to back up the truth of these two doctrines.

The Spiritualist religion does not expect its membership to have *blind faith* that what that they are being asked to believe in is the truth, but on the contrary, they encourage their members to base their faith on the evidence being offered to them.

This evidence is being demonstrated at every Spiritualist church throughout the world, week in, week out. In addition to the many Spiritualist organisations, there have been hundreds of books written on the subject. These books can be obtained from your local library, or on the internet.

I hope I have been able to make this book on how I became a Spiritualist interesting and enlightening but more importantly, I sincerely hope that you will consider it worth examining the subject further.

If you do take the trouble to look into Spiritualism further, I believe it is possible that you, too, can find the peace of mind and understanding of life that I have enjoyed ever since I made that first trip into Grays Spiritualist centre all those years ago.

I wish you all, Love and Light. Paul Shave.

APPENDIX

I think it may be helpful to you, dear reader, if I explain some essential things to bear in mind when witnessing a communication from the world of Spirit in a Spiritualist church or a private one-to-one sitting. To do this, I have used the words of wisdom given to me in my first two articles that I wrote for the Institute of Spiritualist Mediums; both articles, I believe were inspired from my spiritual helpers on the other side of the veil.

ARTICLE 1:
RECEIVING A MESSAGE FROM A MEDIUM

It is well to remember when receiving a message from a medium that it is always in the nature of an experiment in that several conditions need to be in place. The medium needs to be comfortable with the conditions that they find themselves in so that they can relax and tune in to the higher vibrations of the Spirit World. Whilst the medium is so engaged, our friends on the other side of the veil are making their arrangements for contact to be made between the two worlds.

In their case, they have to lower their vibrations so that they are in harmony with those of the medium. This is not easily achieved as it is the result of practice and development on both sides. There are some further considerations to be taken into account when contact has been established. For instance, is the medium clairvoyant or clairaudient, or both? In the case of a medium using clairvoyance, less than good conditions can impede their ability to see and interpret the signs they are receiving correctly and the same difficulty applies to the clairaudient medium who is trying to hear clearly what is being said by the communicator. A medium with both gifts has a double challenge to overcome, because messages can be a mixture of the two.

Let us assume that all of the above conditions have been achieved and that the medium has established a really good link with their spirit helpers. There are still some further things to be taken into account for a successful message to be received. I think the main one is that of emotion. It is very easy to forget just how much our feelings can interfere with our ability to speak.

We human beings are very emotional creatures and the greatest emotion of all is love. Now consider and picture a mother in Spirit who has for the first time been given the opportunity to speak to a loved one on the Earth plane via a medium. Her love and excitement at the prospect of letting her loved one know that she is still alive and well and still loves them is an emotion so powerful that it could well affect her ability to speak, let alone give her name etc.

Perhaps the most important fact to remember when considering mediumship is that not only do conditions have to be favourable, but also that mediums cannot just call up a particular person to communicate with. They have to work with those who wish to come through, having been given the opportunity. A further thing to be remembered when considering communication from the realms of Spirit is that the mediums and their helpers are still fallible human beings. The guides and helpers in the Spirit World are not perfect although they are, of course, further along the road of development and knowledge than are we on the Earth plane.

It is never easy conveying messages when conditions are good, let alone when they are less so and it is quite a challenge to give only what is being given without adding bits of information of doubtful accuracy out of wanting to please.

The best way I can conclude this consideration of the difficulties of mediumship and the sometimes less than accurate messages received is to quote one of my guides. He said the following words to a person who had just received a very evidential message but still asked why certain things had not been mentioned: "YOU MUST REMEMBER THAT WHEN WE PASS TO SPIRIT, WE ARE STILL IMPERFECT BEINGS. THE INSTRUMENT BEING USED IS ALSO IMPERFECT. ONLY GOD IS PERFECT. SO WHY DO YOU EXPECT A PERFECT MESSAGE?"

ARTICLE 2:
FURTHER THOUGHTS ON RECEIVING A MESSAGE FROM A MEDIUM

In my previous article, I dealt with the conditions that need to be in place before a satisfactory communication can take place. I wish to take the subject of mediumship a little further and also the type of message that the sitter hopes to receive.

Let us deal with the sitter first. Is he or she expecting to be told how to live their life and whether or not they will win the lottery etc. or are they really more interested in hearing from loved ones to help them come to terms with there loss? If it is the former, there are plenty of psychics about who can satisfy their needs. If, however, it is the latter, they will need to seek out a medium who has developed their gift to the level that they are able to be in contact with Spirit. Many of you will know the difference between psychic ability and properly developed mediumship, but for those who don't, let me explain:

A psychic person is one who has a natural gift that makes them aware of information coming to them in addition to their normal five senses. It sometimes comes from the sitter's aura that the psychic can see and read and interpret, or it may come from an item the sitter has given them to hold. This can be a watch or a ring or indeed any item that has been in close contact with the sitter. The information received in this manner can be quite detailed and accurate. However, it is not coming from our spirit friends.

The person with these psychic gifts is not in the strict sense a medium but could in many cases, with the right training and personal dedication, learn to develop their gift and become a good medium and channel for spirit communications.

Mediums are also people with psychic awareness but have dedicated themselves to develop their gift to achieve a higher level where they become aware of the spirit vibrations and are able to receive information, whether it is from loved ones or guides and helpers.

Mediums, it must be remembered, are human beings and will vary in their abilities just like any other people in any other profession. It will depend on their dedication to their own development and to what degree they have the gift of mediumship that will decide the quality of their work. A good communication will also depend on the love and understanding being shown by the congregation or individual sitter.